Introductions in
Feminist Theology

8

Editorial Committee

Mary Grey
Lisa Isherwood
Catherine Norris
Janet Wootton

Sheffield Academic Press
A Continuum imprint

Introducing Feminist Christologies

Lisa Isherwood

Copyright © 2001 Sheffield Academic Press
A Continuum imprint

Published by Sheffield Academic Press Ltd
The Tower Building, 11 York Road, London SE1 7NX
370 Lexington Avenue, New York NY 10017-6550

www.SheffieldAcademicPress.com
www.continuumbooks.com

British Library Cataloguing-in-Publication Data

A catalogue record for this book is available from the British Library

Typeset by Sheffield Academic Press
Printed on acid-free paper in Great Britain by The Cromwell Press, Trowbridge,
Wiltshire

ISBN 1-84127-250-7

Table of Contents

Preface

It is heart-warming to write a preface to another book in the *Introducing Series,* especially when this is written by a colleague and a friend. Lisa Isherwood is an integral part of this challenging—and increasingly popular—series. As well as being an editor, she has written, with Dorothea McEwan, the continually popular book *Introducing Feminist Theology,* as well as *Introducing Body Theology,* with Elizabeth Stuart. As this is the eighth title in the series, a book on Feminist Christologies is long overdue.

We always knew it would not be an easy task. Not only because in feminist circles this is still a hotly-contested area. Many of us—in Britain, at any rate—remember the energizing debate between Daphne Hampson and Rosemary Ruether at Westminster in 1990 that hinged around the issue as to whether faith in Jesus was incompatible with feminism. In fact the issue 'Can a male saviour save women?' has never disappeared and is in fact the question with which this book begins.

But another factor causes complexities, namely, the diversity of feminist theologies around the world that all now develop rich and sometimes conflicting Christologies. An enormous strength of *Introducing Feminist Christologies* is the painstaking effort to introduce and bring centre-stage non-European voices as key partners in the discussion. And this is always done in full awareness of the damage inflicted on colonized countries of the exporta-tion of a European Christ. Each chapter weaves disparate strands not into a forced harmony, but into an increasingly complex challenge to traditional, classical Christologies that the book claims have never taken into account the voices and experiences of women.

Lisa Isherwood brings to every section of this book her own distinctive brand of passionate and engaged prose. There are passages that are provocative and even shocking. Not everyone will agree with her on every point—including myself! This not only reflects the diversity of contexts of feminist theological writing—and the book ranges through all continents—but the varying loyalties to Church, primary loyalty to one specific community or degree of willingness to take on board the depth of the challenges she poses.

But if there is one motif that shines out of this book it is the longing to enable Christology to emerge from the prison of the past with its negative effects on women and to embark at last with all seriousness on its task of transforming the world. Isherwood has the patience to listen to the links between Christology and the suffering people of the world. Repeatedly she warns from the path of seeking merely individual salvation:

> In other words I am willing to sacrifice salvation for liberation and the kingdom (p. 126)!

For this end we are encouraged to live counter-culturally, live transgressively. Every aspect of this Christology is linked with political action for social justice. Isherwood brings Christology out of ivory tower respectability into the gutters of the city and the hidden spaces where women are still being violated. Lest a reader feel that sacrifice and the Cross are too easily given up or given a totally negative value, I recommend the discussion (p. 101) on Christ and consumerism, where we are told to develop a counter-ethic of self-chosen sacrifice, and no longer into being forcibly impaled on the Cross of the world to prolong some false substitutional patriarchal piety: stalwart self-sacrifice might just catch on!

In her final chapter 'The Feminist Future' her destabilizing method is at its clearest. Isherwood's message is that Christology always moves on, self-critical, inclusive of new voices—in this case, indigenous peoples—facing new challenges courageously, maintaining that the full reality of Christ's incarnation has never been dared by those who profess it (p. 131). If the book downplays a traditional spirituality of worshipping the man Jesus of Nazareth on the one hand, on the other hand it opens up a far more challenging area, daring us to uncover yet further dimensions of Christology, and to remain 'passionately engaged in the revolution that is our Christian heritage' (p. 130).

This is a valuable contribution to the *Introducing Series* that will be widely-read, appreciated, debated and contested in a diversity of contexts. What its author—and this editor—so passionately longs for is that in its way it will contribute to social justice in society.

Mary Grey
D.J. James Professor of Pastoral Theology,
University of Wales,
Lampeter, UK

Introduction

Christology, and the reality of incarnation that it claims to expound, is at the heart of Christianity. The 'person and significance' of Jesus, as we were told the word signified as undergraduates, is, of course, what Christianity is about. However, a glance at the church history books and tomes about doctrinal development will show that women have not been part of the debate. Indeed, if one accepts a naïve reading of the christological debates, there is very little need for it to be understood as a gendered activity. If we believe that Jesus lived and died and his early followers simply understood who he was and what he was about, and further that they helpfully wrote this clearly in the Gospels, then there are few questions to ask. Indeed, any questions we do ask can be neatly dealt with by reference to the third person of the Trinity, the Holy Spirit, who cleared up any misunderstandings during the early years of the church. This is not a gendered activity at all but is the self-disclosure of God in an ordered and clear way.

Of course, this is not the whole story! Indeed, it is not the story at all. The twentieth century saw major changes in the way we understand Christology and the ways in which we approach study of the subject. It was Albert Schweitzer[1] who showed that each portrayal of Jesus says more about the scholar than about the man Jesus. From being a damning indictment this has almost become a matter of necessity, certainly in the area of liberation theology. We no longer believe that one, pure and unsullied picture of Jesus can emerge and we have, in most quarters anyway, faced the fact that we can find few authentic words of Jesus in the Scriptures.[2] Christian history is littered with accounts of those who had doubts about the picture of Christ being presented in their day, and in many cases sadly, our history is also littered with their bodies. However, there has perhaps not been a time in history quite like our own, when the christological debate is so wide open and therefore, in my opinion, so enriching and exciting.

---

1. Albert Schweitzer, *The Quest of the Historical Jesus: A Critical Study of its Progress from Reimarus to Wrede* (London: A. & C. Black, 1922).
2. The work of the Jesus Seminar has placed this view firmly in the scholarly arena.

We accept that Christ as preached from the pulpit is an amalgam of many pictures, not always complementary, that are found in the scriptures and during the first century of Christianity. We happily digest the pre-existent Logos of John's gospel and the virgin birth of Matthew's and add it to Paul's notion of atonement, but we do not question in the gaps, we leave the spaces unfilled and begging the questions that we do not always dare to ask. Why was it that not all writers found it necessary to speak of virgin birth and divine conception? Indeed, the author of the Gospel of Philip found such an idea morally outrageous since the spirit was imaged as female and the notion that two women could conceive was not only laughable but also obscene. Paul never speaks of virgin birth, and so it does not seem to be necessary to do so in order for his ideas about atonement to hold true; this is no pure sacrificial lamb that is necessary, as later commentators sometimes assumed.

Adherence to orthodoxy was not a major concern of the very early movement but it did take on significance when Constantine made Christianity the official religion of the Roman Empire in the third century. From that time on Christology became as much an act of domination as one of the revelation of divine truths. The Romans believed it would be easier to rule peoples who held common systems of belief and the church suddenly discovered heretics. The radical message of equality got lost under a new hierarchical bureaucracy. Christ was placed in the hands of power brokers and the broken rabbi on the cross became Christ triumphant, the imperial Christ of conquest and genocide.

It is as difficult to rescue this figure as it would have been to take the man Jesus down from the cross. There have been guardians of this imperial image whose might has been greater than that of the Roman guard on Calvary. This signifies the power of the image and the gains thought to accompany the control of it. Ironically, the image that has been most enduring is that placed in the Nicene Creed an image that is, for the most part, non-biblical.

Appeals to the man Jesus have, as has been mentioned, proved to be illusive. He, from the evidence we have and the greater understanding of first-century Judaism that is emerging, was quite eclectic in his engagement with the religion of the day. There appears to be little that is original to the man Jesus as was once so uncritically assumed. Dominic Crossan[3] sees Jesus as a shrewd peasant teacher who dared to challenge the existing social order, but he does not think that Jesus understood himself as the centre of the message he proclaimed. His message was that people should engage with the liberating God in a more direct way. Of course, Crossan, like everybody else, is reading sparse evidence

3.   See John Dominic Crossan, *The Historical Jesus: The Life of a Mediterranean Peasant* (San Francisco: HarperSanFrancisco, 1992).

through the lenses not only of time but also gender, privilege, education and power—not only within the texts but within his own life.

It is worth mentioning the obvious, which is that the texts themselves took form in a world with totally different mental constructs from our own. This was not just a world of different beliefs but quite different ways of arriving at and shaping those beliefs. It was, for example, a world in which gods and angels walked on the earth. The worst excesses of Greek dualism had not by then taken total hold. There are hints in the Christian scriptures that show how flexible the human/divine boundaries were considered to be. In Acts we read that Paul and Barnabas were at different times thought to be Zeus and Hermes (Acts 14.10-13), while Paul was declared as a god [Acts 28.6]. Therefore, we need to keep in mind that titles like God and Son of God were spoken in a different world than our own.

The early writers each grapple with the stories attached to the life of Jesus in their own way and come to different conclusions. It was not their intention to come to one orthodox position but rather to engage with what had been understood as redemptive praxis. The Gospels agree that Jesus met a terrible end, yet the writers still insist that there is something about his life worth taking note of, that by paying attention to him they could in some way change their world.

Much contemporary Christology is concerned with how one's understanding of the life of Jesus can help transform present circumstances; in other words it looks less to how Jesus has already saved us and more to how we may be empowered to fight for change. Feminist Christology sits right at the heart of this liberative approach and is pushing the boundaries in all directions. Contrary to some popular opinion it still engages with the stories concerned with the life of Jesus, but this is not always the first step. The lived reality of the lives of women and men is the starting point and then biblical stories and other forms of literature are added to the reflection in order to find ways ahead. In short, it is not assumed that simply 'reading' the life of Jesus from the Scriptures is either possible or beneficial. If it were possible, living the life of a first century rabbi/itinerant preacher in the twenty-first century may not make the world a better place.

Feminist theology has changed during the course of its short history. Its detractors assume this means it is indecisive, while its practitioners understand the flexibility of the model to be its strength. Indeed, any theology that is going to declare the lived experience of people to be the starting point for its reflections has to be flexible and will change. This is, of course, in stark contrast to theologies that begin with 'absolute reality' and immovable metaphysics.

It goes without saying that the faces of Christ will also change according to context, and this is one of the exciting movements in the current feminist theological scene. Having recovered from a predominantly white middle-class start, feminist theologies now embrace a rainbow of experience, and consequently the Christ that is emerging is more inclusive and challenging than possibly at any time in christological history. Diversity is now celebrated and not silenced by the hand of conformity. This is not to suggest that hierarchical theological dinosaurs embrace the changes and some still try to bring destruction in their plodding wake. However, feminist theologies continue to flourish and the Christ who is emerging speaks deeply and challenges creatively those who can hear and act in a diverse world.

Feminist theologies are, of course, affected by postmodern and postcolonial discourses, and so the sands are ever shifting. Why this should be so shocking to a religion whose God committed to flesh is a mystery. The only guarantee of unchanging absolutes lies in the realm of philosophy and the rigidity of patriarchal thinking that underpins it. Life is just not like that! Indeed, the lived experience of women and men from around the globe tells us that the rigidity of Christian dualistic thinking has to change because it has caused them harm. The Christ of conquest who was exported with soldiers and missionaries was made in the image of the conqueror and the results were devastating. With neat divisions of higher and lower life forms in place, the colonial Christ relegated indigenous peoples to the bottom of the pile where they could be abused and exploited. The stories are, of course, different according to the exact setting but a general understanding can be grasped. Christianity, as an accompaniment to conquest, viewed its role as that of civilizing, for which we may read westernizing, those peoples it encountered on its global march. The result was loss of culture, religion, symbol systems and self-esteem, not to mention land, human rights and dignity. The indigenous population of Latin America was almost wiped out in the space of ten years through violence and diseases. While the inhabitants of the Philippines, who had a culture that respected women, felt the full force of patriarchal religion, the women being reduced in status and dignity. While I am not arguing that Christianity walked into paradise and converted it to hell, or that every culture in the world, except western ones, respected women and saw them as equal, I am suggesting that Christianity played into many of the worst aspects of existing cultures as well as imposing its own brand of dualistic hierarchy. Also, as can be expected when the position of the men folk in a society is reduced as it was through colonial rule, then the position of women will also worsen. Indeed, women usually find themselves at the bottom of the heap, bearing the brunt of the oppression of their men.

Postcolonial discourse is then not only important to theology because it highlights the injustices carried out in the name of the colonial Christ but because it brings new ways of thinking into theology. Christ is removed from the pedestal of imperial overlord and examined anew through the philosophical and cultural constructs that he, as part of the colonial venture, suppressed. When Chinese women engage with Christ they do not use the dualistic thought of the west, since for them negative and positive are part of the same construct and cannot be divided in the neat, yet unrealistic way, that the west has employed. When African women approach Christology they cannot do so separated from the land or their own understanding of healing and exorcism.

Feminist Christology, wherever in the world it is found, places that which is named as divine at the heart of creation and at the heart of people's lives without the veil of dualistic thinking. This is far too rich a mix for some who prefer the comfort of what we might call 'cataract Christology', a Christ whose demands for radical equality are viewed dimly and as if from afar. And the cause of this reduced vision?—the layers of hierarchy that spawn divisions based on race, class, orientation and other characteristics that have thickened the lens and blocked liberative vision.

This book attempts to chart a course from the early questioning of the relevance of a male saviour to women through the many faces of Christ that have emerged from the lives of women to a place of reflection about the nature of christological thinking in the twenty-first century. It does not claim to be definitive since this is not the stuff of feminist theology, but I hope that it raises questions that move us forward.

Chapter One

Can a Male Saviour Save Women?

As the early proponents of feminist theology strove to understand the exclusion of women and women's experience in church practice and theological reflection, even in churches that had a strong social gospel, they were increasingly faced with the realization that it may be the very fabric of Christianity that caused the exclusion. It was not so easy simply to point to current cultural norms and say that Christianity had lost its way and was too deeply embedded in a culture that was essentially opposed to its teachings. The cause of the problem was seen to be much deeper, and it was suggested that the maleness of Christ himself may be part of the difficulty. Traditional belief held that the incarnation and subsequent death and descent into hell were to enable the divine to experience all and therefore redeem all. If Christ could not experience being female then the question was raised as to whether the female state could be redeemed. This was not a new question, and it had occupied the minds of the church fathers for many generations, many of whom could just not believe that women, the descendants of Eve, had been saved in the same way as men. Indeed, it was at one time believed that after the resurrection women would be half male and half angel. The rupture in divine creation would be healed and God's original creation would be restored. It goes without saying that the way in which feminist theologians were now asking the question about Christ as a saviour for women was radically different to that of the fathers. Instead of problematizing women through the question they were exposing the flaws in Christianity. Here was a religion that declared universal salvation yet denied women full participation in all aspects of its life and did so on the basis of a questionable philosophical and theological past. As Elizabeth Johnson so succinctly puts it:

> the idea that the Word might have become female flesh is not even seriously imaginable, so thoroughly has androcentric Christology done its work of erasing the full dignity of women as christomorphic in the community of disciples...as a

logical outcome...women's salvation is implicitly put in jeopardy, at least theoretically.[1]

What is being exposed here is a way of thinking and not just a way of acting. In declaring their full dignity as human beings women were issuing a challenge that would cut deep into the theological framework and confront the ways of thinking that create excluding doctrines as much as the content of the doctrines themselves. Androcentric bias and patriarchal logic are both placed under the spotlight and found wanting.

The Male Problem!

Ruether was concerned to examine where the denial of the female first infiltrated a religion that declared a new social order. She was never an advocate of a blissful matriarchy in our pre-history, but she did believe that there was a time when gender inequality was less devastating than it has been throughout Christian history. She finds the origin of the denial of the feminine in the classical Neo-Platonism and apocalyptic Judaism out of which Christianity was born. Here we find the combination of a male warrior God with the exaltation of the intellect over the body. The alienation of the masculine from the feminine is the basic sexual symbol that sums up all the other dualisms that are mind and body; subjective self and objective world; individual and community; autonomous will (male) and bodily sensuality (female) and the domination of nature by spirit.[2]

The Hellenistic influence has shaped concepts such as Logos and Christ in devastatingly androcentric ways.[3] While Christianity has never claimed that God was literally male, the Hellenistic underpinning has led to many assumptions about the nature of God and normative humanity. There has been an unspoken, yet enacted, androcentric bias, which has reduced the place of women and men in the world, holding them as it does to very outmoded and reductive notions of humanness. While these ideas have affected both sexes, women have suffered more assaults on their humanness than males. Augustine even declaring that in our femaleness we cannot be redeemed, while men can

1.   Elisabeth Johnson, *She Who Is: The Mystery of God in Feminist Theological Discourse* (New York: Crossroad, 1992), p. 151.

2.   Rosemary Ruether, 'Motherearth and the Megamachine: A Theology of Liberation in a Feminine, Somatic and Ecological Perspective', in Carol Christ and Judith Plaskow (eds.), *Womanspirit Rising* (San Francisco: Harper & Row, 1979), pp. 43-53 (44).

3.   Rosemary Ruether, *Introducing Redemption in Christian Feminism* (Sheffield: Sheffield Academic Press, 1998), p. 82.

be, who possess the image of God in themselves. Women, on the other hand, are defective males who are born as the result of a birth defect (Aquinas). Women are not the full creation that God intended. It follows as a matter of logic from these ideas that the Saviour had to be male and that this has certain implications for women. At each turn in the Christian narrative women are systematically excluded or defined as inferior. Indeed, much of the Christian story depends on the 'truth' of women's inferiority, since the logic of many of the doctrines, such as atonement and redemption, spring from an understanding of Eve and so-called Original Sin. Without the weakness and deceit of the original woman there would be no need for a redeeming saviour. God's secondary act of creation, Eve, brought about the need for a whole new creation, which was initiated through the perfect son of God, the God/man, who sets the record straight. Woman, then, has a place but a rather disruptive one; she proves herself to be untrustworthy from the start and has to be viewed with suspicion. How then can this creature be redeemed? The question is a real one and the answers have been varied and have carried a variety of consequences for women, from the grotesque to the merely ludicrous. Simply by refusing to believe the rhetoric of the innate inferiority of women, feminist theologians are bringing into question the entire androcentric/patriarchal logic that has to date underpinned christological debates. The question is, can Christology exist without such androcentrism?

It is quite clear that under such a system it is virtually impossible to work out the basic conviction that women are human beings and are in the image of God. According to Ruether the dualism of patriarchal religion is not the only aspect that discourages us from claiming our own divinity and redemption. She says the 'parent model' of the divine confronts us with a neurotic God who does not want us to grow up.[4] Indeed, to become autonomous and responsible is a great sin, while spiritual infancy is a virtue. This is in part true for all Christians but is emphasized for women who have to place themselves in the hands of, until recently, male spiritual advisors and under the leadership of male clerics and their husbands. This has never sat well with women, and Christian history is littered with women who wish more autonomy and religious freedom; many have come to tragic ends, while others have found ways to survive within the system yet with some degree of freedom. (Many mystics are good examples of this dance between power and autonomy.) Ruether points out that there was a time when God was far more encouraging in terms of our own freedom, when the business of reminding us of our

---

4. Rosemary Ruether, *Sexism and God-Talk* (London: SCM Press, 1983), p. 69.

divinity included putting down the mighty, releasing captives and vindicating the oppressed. She says: 'If he could be it again he would free slaves, include Gentiles and perhaps even women!'[5] Ruether is quite confident that it can happen again, because with the death of Jesus, the Heavenly Ruler has left the heavens and been poured out on the earth: 'A new God is being born in our hearts to teach us to level the heavens and exalt the earth and create a new world without masters and slaves, rulers and subjects'.[6] There can be no claiming of divinity for anyone while injustice and inequality stalk the earth. Ruether is keen to unleash the human potential bound by patriarchy, because a tradition that promised a prophetic liberating tradition cannot be left in the hands of its perverters, in which it becomes a static set of ideas.

Throughout Christian history there has been what Schüssler-Fiorenza calls 'the egalitarian counter-cultural trend' that has spoken about the equality of women. This trend has usually been connected with ascetic sects that have been condemned as heretical. It would be incorrect to suggest that there have not been snatches of this trend in movements that, while not dominant, escaped condemnation. For example, it comes through in Protestantism in such left-wing utopian and mystical sects as the German Rappists or Shakers, who felt a male Christ was totally inadequate as he could not reveal the female nature of God. Mysticism, with its direct relation to God, has enabled women to have authority and autonomy against patriarchs. The same is true of some religious orders that have valued the gifts of women. However, it was often the case that the dominant tradition and God the Father, Ruler and Judge in time regained his power. Those women who resisted the loss of their privileges were often sent to the stake as vehicles of the devil.

For some kinds of 'deviant' Christianity, equality in Christ did actually mean a new relationship between men and women within the churches. Montanism and Gnosticism did not scapegoat women but gave them equal prophetic authority and participation in ordinary ministry. Dominant Christianity defended itself by saying that it never denied equality in Christ, but of course this was in a spiritualized way, and therefore the actual nuts and bolts of everyday equality were hardly given a thought. Gnosticism argued it was necessary to transcend our sexual bodily nature, and it felt women could do this as effectively as men. It is sad and ironic that the church, which should be the haven of women's dignity and full humanity, declared heretical those movements that attempted to acknowledge these truths.

Despite these encouraging historical moments the church has a long record

---

5.   Ruether, *Sexism and God-Talk*, p. 3.
6.   Ruether, *Sexism and God-Talk*, p. 11.

of abuse of women. It may therefore appear difficult to find a usable past since everywhere we turn we see pictures of our unworthiness, guilt and inequality. Further, if we take a once and for all view of Christian revelation that picture is hardly likely to change. Letty Russell is among those who believes that liberation theology does offer women a way to find a usable past, although she acknowledges the difficulty faced in dealing 'creatively and faithfully with tradition'.[7] She argues that there is ample biblical evidence that illustrates that a completed and therefore static view of revelation was a late addition to Christianity, one that flies in the face of Jesus' promise of the Spirit that will lead people forward (Jn 16.13). Russell demonstrates that none of the so-called infallible traditions have actually been cast in stone by the divine. She illustrates her point by referring to the way in which the divine was imaged in the Hebrew Scriptures. God is often referred to in female terms and three of the most important ideas in Judaism are spoken of in the female. These are Shekinah (glory of God), Chokmah (pre-cosmic deity), Torah and (laws of guidance). The female nature of these ideas was downplayed over the centuries, which illustrates Russell's point that things do change. Therefore feminist theologians may either change them back or look for new ways forward. She says,

> the heresy of our time is not that of re-examining the Biblical and ecclesial traditions. It is the refusal of the Church to hear the cry of oppressed people and to speak and act on behalf of liberation for all.[8]

Interestingly, those who we in the west may view as falling into Russell's categories of the oppressed do not always have the same problems as we do with the maleness of Christ. Indeed, in certain cultures it is a positive advantage that Jesus, a man, could concern himself with women at all. For example, Filipino women do not find the maleness of Jesus to be a problem in their Christology. Indeed, as he was born a male he was in the best position to challenge the male definition of humanity and male privilege. He could offer a more affective challenge to men to change their ways. Many do, however, have certain problems with culture. There have been many moves in liberation theology to develop more culturally appropriate models of Christology, models that grow out from the resident culture and thus sit well with it. However, in a patriarchal society this does not necessarily fill women with joy. Much effort has to be made to ensure that women are allowed to create a

---

7.   Letty Russell, *Human Liberation from a Feminist Perspective: A Theology* (Philadelphia: Westminster Press, 1974), p. 73.

8.   Russell, *Human Liberation*, p. 103.

liberative space in their own culture before 'the cultural Christ' is welcomed with open arms. However, it is clear that patriarchal culture, not the gender of Jesus, is thought to be the most pressingly problematic.

Meanwhile, others, such as Virginia Fabella,[9] believe that the historical Jesus plays a central role in the creation of Christology. Through his works and words, Jesus showed what true humanity and divinity looked like; therefore, it is important to focus on this when seeking liberation in the present. There are any number of problems with this since the kind of historical accuracy that would be necessary to set out an exact way of being is not open to us. Further, to what extent does knowing how a first-century Jew acted help us to act now? The answers have in fact to be generalized and open to a great deal of interpretation, and it is this path that Fabella takes despite her protestations about exploring the historical Jesus. It appears that what she means by the historical Jesus is simply one who changed things in the here and now. For her Jesus' historical importance does not lie in accurately attesting to each action and saying but rather in our history. Despite appearing to acknowledge this, Fabella still falls into the trap of assuming that Jesus treated women in a radically different way from others of his time. Scholars now know that his actions were not as unusual as we have previously thought. We know there were female rabbis and wealthy women merchants who commanded respect and a large degree of equality. Therefore, it could be argued that Jesus was less than radical in his approach to women.

However, it is suggested that Jesus showed what being human meant, and it is this quality of humanness that is needed if one is to enter the kingdom of God. To be truly human one has to live in relation with others and exclude all power relations. Loving one another takes priority over temple worship and serving others is more important than power and prestige. This quality of humanness is open to all and is seen as a pre-requisite of the kingdom. The emphasis on Jesus as the revealer of true humanness in many ways springs from the cultural setting. In Asia there is much interreligious dialogue but far more informal 'dialogue for life' where people

> share the life conditions, pain, risks, struggles and aspirations of the Asian poor (the majority of whom are of other faiths or even of 'no faith')…made us aware of our common search for a truly human life, our common desire for liberation from whatever shackles us internally and externally, and our common thrust towards a just society reflective of what we Christians term 'the kingdom'.[10]

9.   Virginia Fabella, 'Christology from an Asian Woman's Perspective', in Virginia Fabella and Sun Ai Lee Park (eds.), *We Dare to Dream* (Hong Kong: AWCCT, 1989), pp. 109-13.

10.   Fabella, 'Christology', p. 5.

If metaphysics and the infallibility of certain doctrines took centre stage such a dialogue would be severely hampered. However, the historical Jesus, who calls people to humanness, by-passes such problems as well as those of gender. Debates about the divine nature of Jesus are not allowed to hamper the transforming experiences that people struggle for as they act humanly. This has special significance for women in a society that has for so long limited their humanness through restrictive civil and religious practice. To demand human rights could be the christological first step for many women. What is certain is that Jesus has no relevance for women if he is detached from their lives under the weight of metaphysics. Of course, this means that he can never be static and is always open to modification by circumstances. However, this is a powerful element ensuring that Filipino women continue to include him in their struggles.

Monica Melancton also gives a hint as to how some Indian theologians deal with the problems of the maleness and male identification of Jesus. This, she says, is part of the historical Jesus, but it does not mean that it is an essential ingredient of the risen Christ who is dwelling in the redeemed order.[11] This risen Christ transcends all particularities. In this way the maleness of Jesus can no longer dictate the femaleness of all women through time, and he becomes the symbol of a new humanity rather than a model of gender enactments. While this argument may be what is necessary within the Indian context, there are some problems with it. The notion that humanity is an androgynous mass underneath cultural overlays of gender enactment is one that has been heavily criticized. Many feminist theologians, who have no wish to be shackled by the assumptions of essentialism, nevertheless argue that human nature is not androgynous and that many of the differences that we see displayed between the sexes have redemptive significance in themselves. Of course, there is always the danger that in claiming Jesus as the model of 'humanity' we have 'maleness' yet again turned into universal ways of being.

From the perspective of traditional Christology this raises the question of the degree of Christ's humanness, that is, was he a man or not? If he was fully a man, to argue that he was fully human negates the place of female experience in humanness, and he did not know how it felt to be a woman. If he did somehow experience being both male and female, then he was either trans-gendered or not fully human. Being human is an experience and that experience is, in our day, and was in the time of Jesus, a gendered experience. However, this argument is not of primary importance in the Indian context

11. Monica Melancton, 'Christology and Women', in Virginia Fabella and Sun Ai Lee Park (eds.), *We Dare to Dream* Hong Kong: AWCCT, 1989), pp. 14-22 (18).

where the landscape is one of rigid misogyny. Within that context emphasis on the humanity of Jesus rather than his masculinity is a crucial step forward.

Indian women are demanding that the churches inspired by the example of Jesus should be counter cultural and support them in their struggle for dignity in a patriarchal society. Their Christology then emphasizes that Jesus was a saviour for women within their own patriarchal situation. He did not judge them by the standards that their society set, for example, he did not condemn the adulteress or shun the Samaritan woman who had many husbands. He healed them even when their illnesses would have made him unclean in the eyes of his society. Also, and crucially, he did not exclude them from what might be seen as the 'deeper things', for example, his teaching and the revelation of his being. The women around Jesus, it is argued, actually understood his significance more easily than the male disciples and tended to his needs more than his male colleagues were able to. They remained faithful when others fled. Jesus reached out to women and they to him in a mutual embrace of recognition and respect. It is this image that Indian women theologians find most powerful.

It is this Christ who they hope will stem the tide of dowry brides, temple prostitution and widow burning. It is perhaps only this Christ who can begin to balance the mortality rate, which reflects the fact that far more female babies die from neglect than should be the case. Many more are not even reaching birth since mobile scanners have made it possible for women in villages to know the sex of their child before birth and many are succumbing to the pressure to abort. Indian Christian women place their hope in the woman-loving Christ to raise the literacy level among women and to gain more stable employment rights for women. They also hope that rape and physical abuse both inside and outside the family will decrease. Of course, Christ will not do this through magic but through the realization that Jesus thought that women were human too and deserved the dignity and celebration attached to all God's creation. It is the male Christ who acted against 'male culture' who gives hope to many women in India. The message of women's dignity is more powerfully heard when spoken by a man within that culture. Jesus then is the male advocate par excellence and his gender is less of a problem than his colonial crown.[12]

For many feminist theologians, then, the 'scandal of particularity' is no scandal at all. That Jesus was a first-century male son of a carpenter and the son of the eternal God sits easily with some. As we see with the work of

12. For more on the colonial Christ see Lisa Isherwood, *Liberating Christ* (Cleveland, Ohio: Pilgrim Press, 1999).

theologians from the Philippines and India, the 'problems' are thought to be overcome by the assertion that Jesus was a man quite unlike others of his time and culture, that is, he embraced women and included them in his message. Ruether is not happy with this solution, since she believes that we do have to admit the particularity of Jesus and deal with it. She reminds us that classical Christology has prided itself on the dissolution of all particularity, and look where that has got us. She says:

> I believe we should encounter Jesus, not only as male, but in all his particularity as a first century Galilean Jew. We then must ask how we can see him as paradigmatic of universal human redemption in a way that can apply to female as well as male, to people of all ethnicities and cultures.[13]

Ironically, this approach shifts the emphasis from the biological importance of Jesus as based in theology that springs from Hellenistic influences to his message. Jesus was the embodiment of that message and it is in this way that his physical being becomes important. However, women and men can embody the message in the same way and so this expands the scope of message and redemptive action. Ruether frees us from biological determinism and spiritual infancy in one majestic move. By prioritizing the message and not the gender Christians become 'redemptive community not by passively receiving a redemption 'won' by Christ alone, but rather by collectively embodying this path of liberation in a way that transforms people and social systems'.[14] The Christ who is to come is then understood to be 'the fullness of all this human diversity gathered together in redemptive community'.[15] This understanding of Christology does away with patriarchal order and integrates an equalitarian understanding of human nature into Christology.

There are other feminist theologians, such as Mary Daly, who would not perhaps be as contented as Ruether is with this approach. For Daly Christianity is irredeemably patriarchal, and so for her the notion that women should wish to be redeemed through it and within it is a mystery beyond all comprehension. Not only is it a mystery, it is impossible. Patriarchy rests on the precise, so beautifully expressed by Daly herself, that 'if God is male, then male is God', so why would men wish to give up such privilege? Indeed, how can they since it is within the fabric of all aspects of western culture? It is within the fabric because it is embedded in the language we use and the modes of thinking that we employ. Lacan images women as absence, basing his

13. Ruether, *Introducing Redemption*, p. 93.
14. Ruether, *Introducing Redemption*, p. 93.
15. Ruether, *Introducing Redemption*, p. 94.

observations on female genitalia, which he considers to be nothing more than a hole waiting to be filled,[16] while Irigaray who wishes to counter such accusations has to agree that women are absent in all aspects of western culture. Therefore, to go beyond God the father and the world of the sons that he spawns, requires more than the addition of women to the equation in a western mind set that finds it hard to go beyond woman as passive space. Ruether, of course, is not suggesting this simple formula, but it could well be argued that unless the male is for a while removed from the picture, his very existence will inevitably lead to a backward move to patriarchy. Daly tends towards a separatist approach in matters of theology and religious language. Indeed, she has attempted to create a new language that is free of all patriarchal bias, and her recent books have been awash with gynocentric passion and expression.

Daly proposes the castration of Christianity through the removal of the products of supermale arrogance,[17] namely, the myths of sin and salvation. Both hold women captive and both lend themselves to scapegoating not only Jesus but also those who fail to model themselves on this illustrious hero. Women, of course, are doomed to fail because of their distinct nature; the Christ image has legitimated sexual hierarchy throughout Christian history. This stands as a reminder to those who would avoid christological difficulties through universalizing, particularizing, trivializing or spiritualizing the person of Jesus, that people suffer according to the Christ we image. All this is, according to Daly, Christolatry, a worship of false gods. What we need to remember is that nothing is neutral in Christology, and so attempting to soften the edges will not ultimately work.

Daly still has use for some of the language and ideas inherent in the Christian story but characteristically she develops the meaning in a gynocentric way. She looks forward to the Second Coming, which will not be the return of the Christ but the emergence of female presence, a presence that will 'liberate the memory of Jesus'[18] through female pride and self-affirmation into a place of contagious freedom. This freedom will extend to all and not make female experience into metaphysical absolutes.

So does Daly think that a male saviour can save women? Well, of course not, but she also introduces the notion that Jesus may need women to redeem

16. Jacques Lacan, 'Jacques Lacan and the Ecole Freudienne', in Juliet Mitchell and Jacqueline Rose (eds./trans.), *Feminine Sexuality* (London: Macmillan Press, 1982).

17. Mary Daly, *Beyond God the Father: Towards a Philosophy of Women's Liberation* (London: Women's Press, 1986), pp. 71-72.

18. Daly, *Beyond God the Father*, p. 96.

him, to free him from the chains of male arrogance and the tendency to scapegoat, a tendency that we see first in the early pages of Genesis!

Atonement Theology and the Abuse of Women

The image of a son sacrificed to his father in order that good may come of it is a common theme in masculinist mythology. These stories tend to establish a bond between the father and son, who may previously have been portrayed as rivals. In short they are stories about male bonding and fathers teaching sons invaluable lessons about the role of the hero and the glory of sacrifice. Christianity has such a story at its very heart and has spoken of it as the tale of universal salvation. Not unsurprisingly women have struggled in this heady world of male bonding and have found themselves to be alienated by the story or victimized by it. Women have found that their lives do not speak of sacrifice and suffering as salvific but rather as crushing of the very humanity they strive to rejoice in. The cross and atoning interpretations placed on it have, then, proved problematic for women over the centuries and no less so for feminist theologians in the last 30 years. Reflecting as they do upon the lives of women as starting points for theological reflection, they have concluded that theories of atonement have made women into victims.

Womanist theologians were amongst the first to engage critically with the notion of glorious sacrifice. Coming as they do from a situation where slavery is a recent memory, they were suspicious of doctrine that appeared to justify suffering and death. Delores Williams[19] is adamant that the cross legitimizes the surrogacy experience of black women, that it makes the bearing of other people's burdens legitimate when in fact it is inhumane. She says: 'The cross is a reminder of how humans have tried throughout history to destroy visions of right relationships that involve transformation of tradition and transformation of social relations and arrangements sanctioned by the status quo'.[20]

As Christians black women cannot forget the cross, but they would be unwise to glorify it as this could make their exploitation sacred. The whole notion of the sacrifice and death of Jesus has been a tricky one for womanists, many of whom acknowledge that their foremothers found great comfort in

---

19. Delores Williams, *Sisters of the Wilderness: The Challenge of Womanist God-Talk* (Maryknoll, NY: Orbis Books, 1993).

20. Delores Williams, 'Black Women's Surrogate Experience and the Christian Notion of Redemption', in William Eakin, Jay B. McDaniel and Paula Cooey (eds.), *After Patriarchy: Feminist Transformations of the World Religions* (Maryknoll, NY: Orbis Books, 1991), pp. 10-22 (12).

the idea that Jesus could save then from their suffering through his own. There is a tightrope to be walked here and the debate is far from over. A significant newcomer to this debate is the phenomena of the Promise Keepers. This is a largely African American group of men who have repented of their waywardness and have returned to their families in order to provide 'headship'. One significant result of this has been an increase in domestic violence. This should not surprise us since they have returned with a very hierarchical and authoritarian understanding of what male headship in a Christian family should look like. This has, of course, given womanist theologians more to ponder on and they are beginning to address the kind of muscular Christianity that leads to abusive situations. Of course, the urgency of addressing the suffering servant brand of theology has also been highlighted since it is guaranteed to deliver women into the abusive hands of Christ's muscular fathers and husbands.

Domestic violence is increasingly being brought to light, and it has shocked some that levels of violence are as high in Christian homes as in others. Indeed, in some fundamentalist areas in the United States figures show the levels to be higher than average.[21] There are many reasons for domestic abuse[22] and of course Christianity is not to blame for all of them. However, Christians cannot be complacent about the part that their doctrinal world plays in its continuation. Traditional theologies of the cross present us with a model of divine child abuse and strong obedience and dependency models. These models are not helpful to women in an androcentric world. The supreme example of the suffering of Christ has held many women in abusive situations and numbed the pastoral response of many clerics. Christine Gudorf has demonstrated how the sacrifice of surrogate victims does not interrupt the violence but rather re-channels it, because the perpetrator is protected from the protests of the victim and any consequences for his actions.[23] By ritualizing the suffering and death of Jesus into a salvific act Christian theology has disempowered the oppressed and abused and therefore encouraged the cycle of abuse.

---

21. Susan Brocks Thistlewaite, 'Every Two Minutes', in Judith Plaskow and Carol Christ, *Weaving the Visions: New Patterns in Feminist Spirituality* (New York: HarperCollins, 1989), pp. 302-11. The statistics are taken from the United Methodist Church's Programme of Ministries with Women in Crisis.

22. The latest government report shows that an incident of domestic violence occurs every 17 seconds in the United Kingdom.

23. Christine Gudorf, quoted in Elisabeth Schüssler-Fiorenza and Shawn Copeland (eds.), *Violence against Women* (London: Concilium, 1994), p. 14.

Closely connected with theologies of the cross and the goods of suffering are notions of forgiveness and selfless love. Both these concepts, while completely consistent with notions of salvific death, have proved destructive for women. They have kept women in abusive situations rather than fostering ideas of self-worth that lead to resistance and independence. Being encouraged to love enemies and not resist evil leads to a mind set in which victims remained victimized. Worse still, the damage done to the self-esteem of women leads many to drug and alcohol abuse and suicide.[24]

There is a problem with the notion of self-sacrificing love: it may be a lesson that men need to learn from a male saviour, but it does not save women. Indeed, it dooms many thousand of us annually to patriarchal abuse and death. While we continue to think of the death of Jesus as salvific by its very nature, instead of an outrageous act of public torture and social control, we put the lives of women at risk. The death and resurrection motif may be glorious for Jesus and Rambo but it is crippling for women. We have to move away from such understandings if we are to flourish.

Historical Tyranny versus Feminist Autonomy

Daphne Hampson is concerned about the male Christ for reasons beyond that of biological determinism. For her the central question is one of maturity,[25] and she puts it clearly: 'To be a Christian is to be placed in a heteronomous position. Feminists believe in autonomy'.[26] To be in the position of having another ruling over one is, in her opinion, to be in the role of a child. Women, she believes, have been in such a position under the rule of clerics and husbands due to the way in which Jesus is imaged as saviour. It is a disempowering image and one that leads to lack of personhood in relationships. Feminism, Hampson declares, stands for the full adult equality of women.

Like Daly, Hampson believes that Christianity will never be able to enact such an understanding because it is based in a sexist and patriarchal past. Hampson understands Christianity to be an historical religion in the sense that events from the past influence present-day matters. Why else, she wonders, would people ask what Jesus might have done in similar circumstances to their own? This constant reference to the past makes Christianity a non-viable

---

24. See Lisa Isherwood, 'Marriage Heaven or Hell: Twin Souls and Broken Bones', in Adrian Thatcher, *Celebrating Christian Marriage* (Edinburgh: T. & T. Clark, 2001).

25. See Daphne Hampson, *Swallowing a Fishbone? Feminist Theologians Debate Christianity* (London: SPCK, 1996).

26. Hampson, *Swallowing a Fishbone?*, p. 1.

religion in the present: it is not moral enough for the modern day which is a time when the equal rights of women are acknowledged and the full humanity of all people is championed. While issues to do with women are always considered in the light of a man who lived 2,000 years ago, the way ahead for women is gloomy. Such a man was bound to agree with much that was fundamental in his culture, and therefore women will not find much that is liberating in his message. Hampson takes on the point that Christianity has changed over the centuries but still remains sure that the revelation point in history will always be of significance and therefore always highly problematic for women. By giving our autonomy away in favour of this moment of revelation, we are flying in the face of a feminist way of life. In giving such power to a revelation one is also giving power to those who claim to understand it most fully, the churches. In ways that are quite contrary to feminist thinking, women are placing themselves in unequal power relationships with churches and clerics. Hampson finds this almost unbelievable since feminist ways of relating are quite different.

For Hampson, then, the attachment to the historical moment of revelation as universally salvific means that women cannot be saved by the male Christ that is portrayed. We do not find our own salvation through giving away our autonomy to the historical person of Jesus or the churches. Hampson's position highlights how male hierarchical thinking, for example, the Lordship of Jesus, excludes women from declaring Christ a saviour just as much as the male gender of Jesus. When feminists consider whether or not a male saviour can save women, the question goes beyond the maleness of the man and embraces the male who has been created by generations of fathers and sons in an attempt to gain a firmer hold on power in the world.

But What Are We Being Redeemed From?

Of course we need to ask if we need to be saved at all. Is Daly right that sin and salvation are myths springing from male arrogance? If she is, then can Christian concepts, themselves created by males, be of any use to us? In addition if we have re-imaged the Fall and our notions of atonement in order to encourage women's self-esteem to be restored, then do we need to speak about redemption at all? Is there anything for a saviour, male or not, to save us from? Women perhaps do need to be redeemed from the patriarchal tradition in religion, which has so cruelly damaged us. We must name and reject it. Christian doctrine holds the roots of many present-day subjecting techniques, Eve: raises her head in many ways from some women referring to menstruation as 'the curse' to the government blaming single mothers for juvenile crimes and the national debt. Women have been encouraged to take on guilt, suffering and self-sacrifice, and this situation needs redeeming.

This is a two-pronged redemption since it involves not only rejecting external oppression but equally it means not playing the victim any longer. Women need at times to be redeemed from the sin of passivity, a phenomenon that has two aspects: one is compliance for lack of ability to protest and one is using 'weakness' to manipulate others. Both require redemption since neither leads to a liberated life.

Feminist redemption theories then move us away from the absolutes of some human/divine being having done it all: to an on-going process that requires our full understanding of and participation in the complex business of 'being human'. This requires overcoming the myths of gender construction more than dealing with an inborn and innate ability to sin.

Mary Grey bases much of her feminist redemption theology on the relationality model of psychology of Gilligan,[27] the crux of which is that women develop a sense of self in relation while boys develop a sense of self in isolation and through competition and separation. It is therefore hardly surprising that male theology is concerned with separation and transcendence. Despite some reservations regarding Gilligan's view, for example it could be argued that she reinforces old gender stereotypes, it is an interesting exercise to imagine how redemption would look if we used the categories of relationality and mutuality to try to understand it. Grey argues that the raw stuff of the universe is interrelationality and so why should we as a species act differently? Scientists are now coming to accept the interrelational nature of the cosmos rather than the very competitive and combative model put forward by Darwin. In addition to accepting interrelationality it is important to assert that relation and interconnection are also based on mutuality as it is possible to have both in quite an unequal way of being.

There are two other important components in the life of the cosmos and these are self-renewal, the ability of the earth to recycle and renew itself, and self-transcendence, the ability to reach beyond the present in an evolutionary way. Grey argues.

> If the relational process is at the heart of reality at the heart of the great divine creative-redemptive dynamism, participating in this must be what is meant by holiness. So entering into deeper more meaningful and at the same time juster structures of relating is the kind of redemptive spirituality needed for the

27. See Carol Gilligan, *In a Different Voice: Psychological Theory and Women's Development* (Cambridge, MA: Harvard University Press, 1982).

transformation of the world. Sin must therefore be acting against the relational grain of living.[28]

This involves a creative and mutual connection with nature also. It is surprising that an incarnational religion has been so slow to recognize the place of nature in any rhetoric about redemption. After all we need a space in which to be incarnate and the cosmos itself is infused with this same incarnational energy. The redemptive task towards nature is complex as it means we have to re-envisage the model of legitimate domination that has been placed in front of us in the pages of Genesis. We have to move from seeing matter as dead and machine-like to cultivating a way of relating to the earth that respects its integrity and allows us to work in partnership with it. The Christian notion of stewardship is too weak a model and one that lends itself to harsh intervention.

Grey is adamant that creation and redemption are linked, and therefore, in the light of current ecological destruction, we would be unwise to move away entirely from notions of redemption. It could be argued that these deeply embedded religious motifs can still provide a way of standing outside the current crisis and envisaging a new way, a redemptive way, for the earth and its inhabitants. However, this new way will need to be deeply embedded in the earth and the bodies of those on it. Dualistic metaphysics has brought us to this crisis and will not help us out of it. The Christ of Greek philosophy is in some measure responsible for the destructive ways of thinking that have been developed in the west, and so how can Christ play a part in the redemption of this situation? For Grey and others; as we shall see in Chapter 4, Christ is still central to the process. However, this is no longer a Christ of heroic other-worldly salvation but an entirely new Christ, a Christ fashioned from the earth and women's reflection upon it.

For Grey women also need the redemptive process of self-affirmation. A major step in this affirmation process is remembering. As we have seen this can be difficult within a traditional Christian framework. However, Grey continues to declare it necessary, since through such action we come to realize that a whole world of knowing has been suppressed by the patriarchal structure. Through women's self-affirmation a new world is opened up, one that increases the divine/human relational potential. Despite the doubts of such thinkers as Hampson and Daly, Grey continues to assert the importance of Christ in the process. For Grey self-affirmation and right relation go hand

---

28. Mary Grey, *Redeeming the Dream: Feminism, Redemption and Christian Tradition* (London: SPCK, 1989), p. 35.

in hand, since without an affirmation of self we are not in a position to enter and negotiate right, just and mutual relation. For Grey, as for Carter Heyward, this is the essence of the Christian message and the life of Christ.

Therefore, Grey continues to argue that salvation/redemption are not out-moded concepts but are as necessary today as at the time of Jesus. Salvation, of course, is not dispensed from the great God/hero but is rather painfully striven for in the global community between justice seekers. For Grey the maleness of Jesus is not the major stumbling block because it has no ontological signifi-cance. He was striving for justice and right relation in a male body, as we strive for it in female bodies. Of course, this will provide different challenges but salvation depends on the process and not the biology.

So, Can He?

So can a male saviour save women? The question is more complex than we might at first have thought, and in the hands of feminist theologians it has moved light years from the ponderings of the fathers. The emphasis has changed from the defective nature of women to that of the destructive nature of patriarchy and patriarchal ways of thinking. The maleness of Christ goes far beyond the physical body of Jesus and calls into question the very ground of being. Some feminist theologians appear to be saying that the very fabric of the Christ is no longer moral enough or flexible enough to encompass the rich diversity brought to the christological debate by women. In other words, the Christ experience is male and, when exposed to women's experience, it shows itself to be fundamentally lacking.

The maleness of Christ as imaged through the centuries has damaged women's self-esteem by relegating us to second-class citizens. In addition it has removed from us valuable images of the female divine, which have his-torically led to respect and veneration for women's bodies and ways of being. We can see clearly how this has been sadly lacking in Christianity. The maleness of Christ has removed women from arenas where they could flourish and has instead placed self-doubt and, at worst, self-hatred, at the centre of the lives of many Christians.

It is also true that the maleness of Christ has spawned an understanding of the power of Christ best enacted on the battlefield than in the churches. This has been the great almighty lord who has laid all waste before him. The saving message that was once shared with people through life and praxis became codified into a stick with which to beat those who would not agree with the power brokers. This supreme lord has devastating effects globally, but it is true to say that where the colonial Christ has beaten men, it has crucified women. This understanding of power is not salvific.

So what are women to do? Some of course, like Daly and Hampson, have abandoned the Christian project as one so fundamentally flawed and outdated that it no longer warrants their attention. Others like Carter Heyward[29] and Elisabeth Schüssler-Fiorenza[30] will not hand the power of the rhetoric over to the religious right since they believe there would be devastating consequences for people and the planet. (We will see more of their arguments in later chapters.) They claim that there is enough in the Jesus story to move us beyond the male monologues and into an ongoing christological dialogue in which all are heard. Is this true? Well, that is for you to decide at the end of the book when at least some of the debates will have been examined. If it is true, who saves whom at the end?

29. Carter Heyward, *Saving Jesus from Those Who Are Right* (Philadelphia: Fortress Press, 1999).

30. Elisabeth Schüssler-Fiorenza, *In Memory of Her* (London: SCM Press, 1983).

Chapter Two

Liberating Prophet

It is not surprising to find great emphasis on the liberating power of Christ in feminist theology, since it is a discipline rooted within the diverse discourses of liberation theology. What is, of course, unique is how liberation will look through the lenses of women's experience. The founding fathers of liberation theology failed to recognize that the way in which women are situated in a patriarchal world requires that liberation has many different faces and addresses diverse issues beyond the merely economic. Feminist theologians engage with women's lives and in so doing they expand our understanding of the nature of liberative activity. Christ the liberator does not simply sit outside the fabric of women's lives setting them free, but is rather embedded in the very core of these lives as they daily struggle for clean water, contraception, freedom from domestic violence and so many other things that signal women's justice seeking. What emerges is a picture of Christ the liberator himself becoming liberated by the demands and hopes of women from around the globe. The traditional notions of the almighty one are tested to breaking point in the face of the crushing and genocidal reality that is the lives of so many women on the planet. Such a model will no longer suffice if Christianity is to remain credible in a world where it appears that people try harder than God to bring about justice. The comfort blanket of dualistic metaphysics has worn thin in a world where the causes of injustice are becoming more transparent each day. In these circumstances what is needed is a liberator who will act with the people and not an almighty ruler who offers delayed gratification (heaven) to those who have watched their children die but never lost faith and the desire to worship their loving God. It may be what is needed but does such a figure exist in Christian theology? Can Christ ever be the one?

In the west Rosemary Ruether was among those who declared that Christ was best understood as a liberator, not in the spiritual sense but in real terms in the political and social realm. Aware, as she is, of the demands for justice in the world, she nevertheless set out a biblically based argument for an understanding of Jesus as liberator. She clearly demonstrates how the Christ of the

Judaeo-Christian tradition was a radical liberative figure. Her Christology was developed in relation to a number of events, among them the Second Vatican Council, liberation theology, feminist theology and her nurturing Jewish uncle, the latter being the spur for her to fight the innate anti-Semitism in traditional Christology.

Ruether wished to take seriously the Jewish roots of Christianity and Christian thinking and so was not prepared to merely brush over Hebraic messianic thought with the gloss of Greek metaphysics. Central to Jewish messianic hope was political action, since for the Jews religious and political life was synonymous. Even when their ideas around the kingdom became more transcendent they never lost sight of the importance of politics. In fact they got thrown into sharp relief and adopted a more radical edge. The Messiah was always understood as a political figure that would champion the poor and the oppressed; he would be a king of Israel. Ruether illustrates that, as people became disillusioned with earthly kings, they pushed the idea of the messianic king into the future and, with the dissolution of the monarchy, the idea was pushed further away but never became a metaphysical hope. Of course, with the changed circumstances of Israel in the world, the Messiah also became more warlike as this was considered necessary if the poor and oppressed were to be championed. The messianic kingdom was one with its feet planted deeply in the earth, that is, it was political and social. However, it appears that it was also deeply patriarchal and this is not entirely surprising given the patriarchal nature of much contemporary Judaism and the increased understanding of the Messiah as a warrior king. Therefore, a warrior male who would rule from the pinnacle of an elitist hierarchy would supply salvation. Ruether is insistent that this was a story that developed under the pressure of circumstances and was not the entire Jewish heritage from which Christians could draw.

Further, Jesus did not appear to accept such a hierarchical scheme. He did not evoke Davidic kingly hopes, rather he praised the lowly and outcast for responding to his message while the reigning authorities stay encapsulated in their systems of power. Further, he did not envisage the kingdom as otherworldly, nationalistic and elitist.[1] He envisaged that it would come on earth when basic needs were met and people could live in harmony. In this new community we would not simply be servants but brothers and sisters, thus replacing the old idea of patriarchal family with its inevitable inequalities (Mt. 10.37-38; 12.46-50; Lk 8.19-21). Jesus also declared that God was not speaking

---

1.   Ruether, *Sexism and God-Talk*, p. 120.

in the past but rather speaking now to challenge the Law and its outdated, life-stifling interpretations (Jn 4.10; 8.4-11; Mt. 9.10-13; 18-22; Mk 2.23-28). Ruether argues that once we see Jesus in this light we find a Redeemer for women. She says:

> Jesus, restores a sense of God's prophetic and redemptive activity taking place in the present-future, through people's experiences and the new possibilities disclosed through those possibilities. To encapsulate Jesus himself as God's 'last word' and 'once for all' disclosure of God, located in a remote past and institutionalised in a cast of Christian leaders is to repudiate the spirit of Jesus and to recapitulate the position against which he himself protests.[2]

Against this background the everyday experiences of women become valuable as disclosers of the divine redemptive process, rather than expressions of alienating 'otherness'. Ruether argues that the disciples had not expected such a denouncement of their messianic hopes and patriarchal expectations, and so they began to turn Jesus into a doctrine rather than risk embracing the events of eternal liberation.[3] We can see the beginning of this process in Luke, where Christ becomes a timeless revelation of divine perfection located in the past. The Risen Lord does not live on but ascends into heaven; therefore access to him is only through the official line of apostolic teaching, which only men can administer. Ruether is not entirely surprised by this since, 'the Gospels are written from the perspective of converted betrayers, disciples who know they had been unable to hear the radical character of his message of abnegation of power in his lifetime.'[4] Therefore, we should not be taken aback that the church continues the betrayal of Jesus by using his name as a means of power and domination over other people. A large step towards this continued patriarchization, as Ruether calls it, came with the establishment of Christianity as the religion of the Roman Empire in the fourth century. The political power Christianity gained from this enabled it to reinstate the concept of the Messiah with its roots in kingship. The Christian emperor with a Christian patriarch at his side could be seen as representing the establishment of Christ's reign on earth.[5]

This was a devastating move, particularly for women, and, coupled with the introduction of Aristotelian biology in mediaeval scholasticism, the hierarchy became even more securely established with males seen as normative and

---

2.   Ruether, *Sexism and God-Talk*, pp. 122.

3.   Ruether, *Sexism and God-Talk*, pp. 122.

4.   Rosemary Ruether, *To Change the World: Christology and Cultural Criticism* (New York: Crossroad, 1988), p. 18.

5.   Ruether, *Sexism and God-Talk*, p. 125.

representative of the fullness of human nature. Women, on the other hand, were viewed as physically, morally and mentally defective. Woman's inability to represent Christ therefore became an unchangeable mystery that emanated from the metaphysical plane and the male normativity of both heaven and earth were well established. Given Ruether's investigation we are left to wonder whether Christianity has anything to offer women and whether women can once again find Jesus.

Ruether thinks that there is enough in the tradition that can be liberated to turn patriarchal interpretations on their heads. She views the task as that of struggling with Jesus for the transformation of the world, beginning with an option for the poor and oppressed. For her Christology does a number of things apart from calling us to seek justice. It also makes us recognize the interconnected nature of injustice and admit to the role of dominant ideologies in the perpetuation of injustices. Most importantly, of course, we have to admit that the fullness of the Christ event is connected with the coming of the kingdom. The latter is plainly not here and so Christology has a 'partial' feel, that is, those qualities that we call Christ-like in the life of Jesus are still to come to fullness. Jesus did not fulfil all the expectations, nor did he establish a church that could simply live in the glory of that victory. The expected messiah has not come and to pretend that he has simply helps us to be numbed to injustice and suffering in the here and now. Ruether claims that Jesus can act as a sign of messianic blessedness to those who wish to see him that way, but rightly understood he is one among many who signal that another order is possible, that which we call the kingdom of God.

Ruether challenges Christianity to see the events of Jesus' life as eschatological, as realities towards which we are still moving, and not as historical events that form the base of an established church. The kingdom is not here even though there are moments when the transcendent becomes present in an anticipatory way through justice, liberation and reconciliation. These moments are never more than relative and indeed should not be made absolute. For Ruether, Jesus is not yet the Christ but is a paradigm for hoping and aspiring; Christ is the fulfilment of that hope.

But what are we hoping for? For Ruether we are aligned with the poor, oppressed and marginalized in the hope of liberation; in the hope of the transformation of the world. Jesus, as we glimpse him, was committed to social and political action, the undoing of social evil and aspirations that are expressed in the Lord's Prayer, where the kingdom is imaged on earth and signalled by the meeting of basis needs for all. Jesus saves by calling people to action and requiring them to participate in the struggles against injustice. He was not a once and for all event of ontological salvation but rather the one who propels us towards the Christ that is the paradigm of liberated humanity.

Rita Brock is critical of Ruether, claiming that she places Jesus in the position of a hero, thus disabling his followers. We give away our own power to those we consider heroes, and this is made no better by the fact that we view the hero as benevolent or even the Christ, we are still left bereft of control in our lives. Brock is only too well aware of how dangerous this is and so warns us against casting Jesus in such a role. She is adamant that basing Christology on a historical figure is a mistake, since it confuses the concept with the phenomena.[6] We should be placing the saving events of Christianity in a much broader context than that of the person of Jesus. She understands the shift in feminist Christology to be from seeing Jesus as the focus of redemption to seeing him as the locus of faith. To illustrate her point she looks at the miracle stories, which she does not wish to explain away but to claim them as normative statements about the nature of Christian community. They show clearly what is possible when we are functioning from the level of connection and not operating with a power-over model. In other words they illustrate the liberative power of Christ in relation and the political nature of illness. Healing, then, is not something bestowed by one with power but is striven for by the whole community in a relationship of power equality.[7] It is unwise to give any of this power away.

Mary Grey offers another warning, this time against viewing redemption as simply justice, not that Ruether imagines that a liberating Christ simply delivers justice. Nevertheless, it is worth examining Grey's argument. She says, 'Redemption seeks to transform the world at a deeper level than do the movements for freedom and liberation—yet it must include them'.[8] Redemption carries with it more than social implications, although these will manifest. Our passion for justice increases our participation in the divine creative ground of our existence. As we become more like God so God will become more tangible in the world as the one who unites feeling, energy and action. Is this problematic for women whose God is imaged in such masculinist terms? While involved in our own self-awakening and development we are also in relation to a profounder process, a cosmic energy that enables us to develop our own visionary powers which are beyond gender. Grey realizes this happens in books more easily than in life because we find it hard to transcend

---

6.   See Rita Brock, *Journeys by Heart: A Christology of Erotic Power* (New York: Crossroad, 1988).

7.   There will be more of Rita Brock's erotic Christology in Chapter 3.

8.   M. Grey, *Redeeming The Dream*, p. 87.

the patriarchal categories of spirit and matter that have been imposed upon us, categories that after all are part of masculinist imaging. So it could be argued that the male Christ is preventing liberation. She feels frustrated in her attempts to find meaning, because under patriarchy the concept 'I want does not exist'.[9] Grey is not merely struggling for words here, she is highlighting the depths to which the patriarchal discourse has taken root. Even the language, that we as women have, is colonized by patriarchal logic and andro-centric bias thereby making it impossible for us to express the meaning that we embody through our experiences. We are literally speechless.[10] We are thrown back on to experience and our feelings, which can know more deeply than our minds ever can.

For Grey Jesus shows how growth in connection can present a radical challenge and lead to transformative action. She illustrates that this was an understanding that Jesus himself had to move towards. She suggests that he had three distinctive periods in his own understanding of salvation.[11] The first suggests a young freedom fighter who views everything with urgency. In Lk. 4.18-30 Jesus appears to be identifying with the task of Isa. 61.1-2, creating liberty for the captives and freedom from oppression. There is emphasis on powerful external influences with salvation being something that happens to people. The second phase shows Jesus realizing that salvation involves both the inner and outer person, and therefore he is able to accuse the Pharisees of outward show (Lk. 11.39). He also seems to realize that salvation involves self-knowledge (Lk. 11.52), which leads us to seek forgiveness (Lk. 15) and to live from the level of justice and compassion. Grey says the third phase shows Jesus developing the redemptive task in global terms.[12] We see too that the values of the kingdom are at odds with the values of the world (Lk. 18.17; 17.24) There is also the suggestion that conversion at an individual level is not enough and that what is required is a conversion at a deep and cosmic level. For Grey the redeeming power of Jesus lies in his ability to discover and make manifest 'the divine source of creative, relational energy in a way powerful enough to draw the whole world with him.'[13] Jesus' own vision of this is clearly stated in Jn 17.20-26, where God is pictured as a relational being.

9.   Grey, *Redeeming the Dream*, p. 87.

10.   For more on this see the work of Luce Irigaray, for example, *This Sex Which Is Not One* (Ithaca, NY: Cornell University Press, 1985).

11.   Grey, *Redeeming the Dream*, p. 96.

12.   Grey, *Redeeming the Dream*, p. 97.

13.   Grey, *Redeeming the Dream*, p. 97.

So, for Grey, Jesus as liberator in a political and social sense is not enough. However, this aspect is integral to a much deeper and more embracing process of liberation, one that ties us into the cosmic/divine relationality which is 'resurrection power in the world.'[14] By living this resurrection we release endless creative energy that has the potential for huge change; it is in the change that we find the liberation. Grey understands that Christ is a liberator but she seems keen that we should not, as Christians, throw away some other aspects of our heritage, those that may be considered more spiritual. The spiritual has caused problems for feminist theologians, since it has been the realm that has been appealed to most by those who have wished to reduce the humanity of women in various ways over the centuries. Grey does not fight shy of these issues but still declares that in understanding Christ in purely political terms we lose a very important aspect of what it is to be Christian.

Alluring and Demanding, Comrade

Unsurprisingly, the Christ who is bursting out in Latin America is not simply the classical liberation Christ of the poor. Women have brought new dimensions, such as colour, race and ecology, to understandings of liberation. The observation of the '500 years of resistance' in 1992, that is, the alternative to the glorification of Columbus, highlighted awareness of colour oppression and exposed Christian attitudes to indigenous spirituality. Elsa Tamez from Costa Rica has focused on the need to understand indigenous spirituality rather than adopt a superior position as Christianity has done since its imposition in Latin America.[15] She is working towards a theology of liberation that takes liberating aspects from both traditions while condemning those parts of both traditions that have been perverted and lead to moral enslavement. She is aware that women have to be particularly alert during this process, since both traditions have not treated them with the dignity and equity they deserve. Tamez, then, is looking for the Christ who can critique and be critiqued by the traditions that came before his conquering soldiers. This is quite a radical move and one that feminists worldwide should pay heed to, because there is still an unforgivable tendency by some to see Jesus as the one who put all the previous wrongs right and saved women from stifling cultures.

Nelly Ritchie from Argentina is in sympathy with Tamez's adventure, since her Christ has 'nothing to do with an applied doctrine but with a truth to

14. Grey, *Redeeming the Dream*, p. 97.

15. Elsa Tamez, 'Quetzalcoatl y El Dios Cristiano', *Cuadernos de Teologia y Cultura* ??.6 (1992), pp. 5-13.

discover, with a response which translated into words and deeds, takes on historical truthfulness and liberating force.'[16] This Christ on a 'continent that is bleeding to death' has no interest in private salvation but moves towards the liberation of the whole people. Therefore, the 'white' invaders cannot find solace in a belief that they will be saved while the continent perishes. The task of liberation involves all the people who inhabit the continent and the continent itself. (We will see more of this in Chapter 4 with the work of Ivone Gebara.) Christian is not a defining term but a 'cosmic vision' and as such Christ can no longer be used to disguise reality or to exclude people. Latin American women are dialoguing with Christ from their own reality in search of lines of action that are liberating. For example, the Mothers of the Plaza del Mayo who weep and witness to their missing children embody liberative praxis in their struggle against powerlessness. They are a resurrection people in that they refuse the final triumph of death, which in this case would be silence. They are in a real sense witnessing to a new life simply by being there; the disappearance and probable death of their children has given life to their own struggle and resistance. They witness to hope in the face of fear and despair.

Ritchie argues that we find a powerful example of our capacities by looking to the woman who anointed Jesus. Here was a woman who was condemned and marginalized yet 'she was for Jesus—the Christ—someone who was not afraid to let others know how she felt, who loved unconditionally, who offered what she had, and who anointed him with her life.'[17]

She loved fully and in so doing revealed the Christ to Jesus. Latin America has many such Christs, women who keep going, who scratch out livings in order to feed their children, women who perhaps even sell their bodies in order to get food for their children. These women, then, are no longer to be judged but to be seen as Christ for their loved ones and for us, the more privileged, who can see the fullness of their love. This is not to romanticize the situation or to justify the existence of such dire circumstances. Liberation still requires that they should not have to pay so dearly to love so fully. However, what is graphically illustrated is that Christ is love in its fullness in the midst of the struggle, whatever means are used to carry on.

The Mexican theologian Maria Pilar Aquino is clear that the necessary means for the struggle to be successful is a thorough understanding of the way in which gender oppression operates. This involves a critical analysis of race,

---

16.   Nelly Ritchie, 'Women and Christology', in Elsa Tamez (ed.), *Through Her Eyes: Women's Theology from Latin America* (Maryknoll, NY: Orbis Books, 1989), pp. 79-91 (82).

17.   Ritchie, 'Women and Christology', p. 88.

class and culture as well as economics. Latin American women have fully to understand how their position in society developed in order systematically to resist and change it. Simply engaging with theology will not actually change society; the resistance has to be from many angles and women have to find their own language in all areas of resistance.

Aquino images Jesus as the one who wished liberation for all, and as it is clearly not visible in the lives of women he would encourage that the redemptive process be continued by those who follow him. She is aware that women will have to do this for themselves, as male theologians have not even come close to addressing the problems that women face. She also encourages a closer working relationship with secular feminists, since they have already started the work of social analysis that is crucial to the next resistance in feminist theology. She also calls for more connection with indigenous spirituality and a conscious connection over class and race lines. For Aquino the great lie that the followers of Jesus have to expose, and quickly, is that the current economic system is not the democratizing force that it claims to be. The truth is that it enslaves and dehumanizes a large percentage of the world's population. Aquino wants the 'dehumanized' to find a common voice and expose the grand lie.[18] It is curious that against this background Christ, who has been used to underpin universal claims and absolutist traditions, takes on a role reversal. The Christ who exposes the grand universal lie of advanced capitalism cannot be one who looks himself for universals and absolute power bases. He both critiques and is critiqued by the mass destruction that springs from thinking in universal absolutes.

Ivone Gebara is among those who acknowledge that the time of striving for absolute and universally applicable truth is over. She believes that we all have to name our context and in so doing we then allow connection to be made between us that are far more 'real' than those imposed from outside. She believes that certain themes will emerge from most contexts, as these are the things that unite us as humans. This can of course be criticized on the grounds that it sounds suspiciously like natural moral law, which the Catholic Church has used to its own ends over the centuries. However, the things that Gebara would see as emerging are quite distinct from those of the fathers of the church. Her focus is on a desire to feed our children and to live in peace.

Gebara therefore naturally thinks that Christian theology has to be conducted from the broadest ecumenical base. Christ, then, must not exclude or

18. Maria Pilar Aquino, 'Directions and Foundations of Hispanic/Latino Theology: Towards a Mestiza Theology of Liberation', in Arturo J. Banuelas (ed.), *Theology from a Latino Perspective* (Maryknoll, NY: Orbis Books, 1995), pp. 192-208.

be seen in such a way as to allow those who define him to exert power over others. She has found that by understanding Christ as part of the Trinity her way forward has been easier. He can be seen as part of a basic matrix of life that illustrates the creative power of interconnection,[19] a matrix that exists because of diversity and thrives on it. In this way Christ is also understood as part of the matrix of creation and the diversity inherent in it. By illustrating her understanding of Christ in this way, Gebara highlights that each individual is in a web of relations that includes other people and the earth itself. The Trinitarian Christ is within this strong, yet fragile, web of life.

Gebara's approach is refreshing. It opens up the possibility of growth and diversity. We can say that the web's strength is preserved when all accept diversity and allow it to blossom. However, the fragility becomes immediately apparent when the will to power is exerted. This damages and may even break the web, and all are made vulnerable, although it may take the aggressors a little longer than everyone else to realize it. Christ as imaged by Gebara can never be used as a stick with which to beat others as this is contrary to the interrelated nature of his own existence. Christ as part of the web of life casts a very different face of God on the earth, and we have to dispense with the all powerful, ruling and controlling image as this too disrupts the web. God loses his unilateral power and we are made to accept the reality that all is in process. Therefore, we cannot simply project a future paradise, but have to work for it now and live with the fear and failure as much as the joy and success.

It is inspiring to see how even when Jesus Christ is declared liberator there is always more to the liberation than meets the eye. Male liberation theologians truly believed that they had found the Christ who would free all. Jesus was no longer the one who declared hidden truths that only the initiated could have access to, he was the one who made us fight against oppression that all could see. However, female oppression was not evident to the eyes of the male clergy who formed the cutting edge of the liberation movement. In pointing this out I do not wish to suggest that the women have seen the whole picture or spoken the final word, rather that they have found new vistas of liberation that require attention. The mistake that the men made was to suppose that they had found the answer because their approach did indeed suggest that some answers could be found for the marginalized. In assuming that this was 'the answer' they have made the same mistake that religion has always made. This is regrettable but not exactly unexpected. After all, totally new models are

19. Ivone Gebara, 'A Cry for Life from Latin America', in K.C. Abraham and Bernadette Mbuy-Beya (eds.), *Spirituality of the Third World: A Cry for Life* (Maryknoll, NY: Orbis Books), pp. 109-18.

hard to imagine and develop and so old habits can easily be accommodated despite one's best resolutions.

The Christ of liberation points to the depth of human experience as the place in which we find the divine. Freeing humans into fuller experiences of what it is to be alive and without chains is a task of divine importance. It is a task that can only be fully undertaken by real engagement with people. As Joan Casanas puts it, 'My God is the people, comrade; alluring and demanding'.[20]

This demanding God does not know the answers but is alive in the questions. The women of Latin American alert us to the difficulties in assuming that even the most radical answer is 'the answer' and the final liberation. The world may now be a smaller place, increasingly dominated by global economics, but it is a place that requires a greater spectrum of approaches if liberation is to succeed. A new insight that women have brought to the debate is the realization that liberation is not a once and for all achievement. It is not so much a final destination as a journey with a variety of stations along the way. However, Christ is not some kind of Omega Point or cosmic/divine navigator but a fellow pilgrim, a revolutionary or a victim but always deeply embedded in the reality of the situation and seeking liberative ways ahead. Christ the liberator is always the vulnerable Christ, there is no room in such an image for Disney-like imaginings and inevitable happy endings.

Christ the Namer of the Nameless

In Korea, as in Latin America, Christ is considered to be deeply embedded in the process of women pushing forward for their liberation. According to Ahn Sang Nim, Jesus could not be anything other than a liberating Christ because he came to preach good news to the poor and women are the poor of the world. He is then their Christ. If we are in any doubt about this all we have to do is look at the genealogy of Jesus and there we see that he rejected the prowess that goes with patrilinear heritage and came solely through the body of women. Further, his ministry is one that is involved with freeing women from patriarchal bondage. Ahn Sang Nim gives many examples of how this is done, all of which could be of benefit in other cultures. However, the one that is particularly interesting, reflecting as she does from her own background, is that of the woman who shouted to Jesus, 'Blessed is the womb that bore you and the breast that you sucked.' (Lk 11.27) In his rejection of this and his praise instead of those who hear the word of God and keep it, Ahn Sang Nim

20. Joan Casanas, 'The Task of Making God Exist', in Pablo Richard (ed.), *The Idols of Death and the God of Life: A Theology* (Maryknoll, NY: Orbis Books, 1983), pp. 130-41 (139).

does not see an insult or devaluing of Mary. Indeed, she interprets this as the rejection of the notion that women are simply 'instruments of succession for a family name', which seems to be their role in much of Asia. By going behind the story and understanding that women's worth in her own culture, then as now, was seen in terms of child-bearing, she is able to look with new eyes at Jesus' response. Her conclusion is that Jesus is the one who values women's bodies and does not wish to see them used as sex objects, breeding machines or as fodder for industrial growth.[21] This interpretation offers a strong critique to traditional Christianity, which prefers not to address issues related to Jesus and the sexed bodies of others. It also critiques the way that some Korean men view the bodies of women as providers of comfort, economics and heirs. Asian women were viewed as property to such an extent that they did not even have their own names; they were referred to in relation to their father, then their husband and finally their son. One of the tasks, then, of Jesus the liberator is to give women a name by which she can be recognized and which she can call her own.

Although this naming process of Christ has a specific reality in Korea and China, it is also foundational in most theologies of liberation. Most of the groups who are developing liberation theology from their particular experi-ence would agree that they are nameless but for the names that the dominant culture places on them, nigger, faggot, whore/slut, spik, gook, and so on. There is of course, it is argued, the 'upside' of the naming process, blacks are strong/athletic, women are good at home making/factory machine work, Latinos are very happy and homosexuals are very artistic. The power of naming, when it does not lie in one's own hands, is indeed dangerous. True liberation lies in the beauty of proclaiming one's own name in opposition to a dominant culture that names for convenience and power.

Free at Last! Free at Last!

Womanist theologians are creating images of Christ against the background of a slave history in which Christ was used against them, to keep them obedient and enslaved. White preachers did not preach about the God of liberation, instead they created special catechisms that emphasized the place of black people in slavery as if by divine will. In addition, those black people who were baptized had it impressed upon them that the freedom they gained through this action was purely spiritual and had no bearing on their slave status.

21.   See Ahn Sang Nim, 'Feminist Theology in the Korean Church', in Virginia Fabella and Sun Ai Lee Park (eds.), *We Dare to Dream* Hong Kong: AWCCT, 1989), pp. 30-38.

Despite this conspiracy of silence regarding the more liberative aspects of the gospel, slaves managed to hear another message, one about the God of Exodus, from which they managed to develop their own black Christ of liberation. This was the Christ spoken and sung about in the secret meetings away from the white preachers. The Christ they met there enabled them to name their own situations as abusive and to seek liberation in this life.

Womanist theologians are pointing out that by exclusively concentrating on race black theologians have overlooked the crucial elements in any liberative struggle, those of class, gender and sexual orientation. Just as in the Black Power movement so in black theology the liberation of black men set the agenda. It has to be noted that in the early days of the struggle many black women did not wish to deflect attention from what they also perceived as the central issue, black power. They were anxious that the whole liberation movement would be discredited if the black community appeared divided by sexism. However, the womanist movement realizes and proclaims that black women are in 'double jeopardy', at least, since they are oppressed members within an oppressed group. They may be in triple jeopardy if they are also poor, as is the case for many. This realization has caused womanists to search for liberation in and through a politics of wholeness, which has led them to criticize the 'haves' both in as well as outside the black community. Those within the black community are understood as sustaining a white way of life that is harmful to their poorer black sisters and brothers. The commitment to wholeness has also led womanists to challenge heterosexism, which has often been rife in black theology, and black churches where homosexuality has been thought of as a white disease. The womanist movement challenges both the sexism of black theology and the racism of feminist theology. It has recently, due to its commitment to a politics of wholeness, sought to do this by siding with the oppressed of colour from around the world. This work is mostly done through EATWOT and is a concrete expression of the theory that no woman is free until all women are free. Therefore, to a certain extent, womanists are beginning to address issues of global oppression, that their brothers failed to grasp. It is against this background that Christology is being explored and developed.

Those who have done the most explicit work on Christology are Jacquelyn Grant and Kelly Brown Douglas. Naturally any womanist appreciation of Christ begins with a recognition of the many-layered oppression under which black women labour that is coupled with a determination to break free. There is also a double-edged approach to black culture from a womanist perspective, that is to say, that women are more critical of it than the men tended to be.

While praising and valuing the parts of it that are liberating and affirming, womanists are also aware that some parts are destructive. Each so-called authentic black experience has to be measured against the vision of wholeness that womanism holds out for the community. Underpinning this vision is the firm knowledge that all are created as valued and loved creatures in the sight of God. All, therefore, have to affirm this by the way they act towards each other within the community. Christ is active in the black community by calling it to rid itself of anything that is divisive or oppressive.[22] This is true in the religious realm as much as the secular, Douglas tells us:

> In regard to Black religion, a religio-cultural analysis challenges any aspect of Black faith that perpetuates the discrimination of particular segments of the Black community. For instance, the ways in which the Black church uses the Bible in the oppression of women, gays and lesbians will be confronted.[23]

Womanists are able to define the black Christ as female as well as male. Anyone who works for the community to liberate it from external and internal slavery and oppression can be seen as the face of Christ. Therefore, Harriet Tubman or Sojourner Truth may reflect the face of the black female Christ.[24] Christ is performative in womanist theology, that is to say, what he did and what others do in following him is more important than who he was in a metaphysical sense. Therefore, actions aimed at creating wholeness are those that are most liberating, most Christ-like. However, Christ the judge is present in the faces of the most disadvantaged black women who call others to continual accountability.[25] They are not calling for repentance alone but for liberation from their crushing circumstances, which requires action on their behalf by those who are part of their problem. This, of course, needs to be understood in the broadest as well as the most specific sense and so is a call to examine global capitalism among other things.

Grant maintains that black women do their theology out of a tri-dimensional oppression, that of class, race and gender. As a result of their gender and their race, they make up a disproportionate number of the poor.[26] However, it is interesting to note that there are more whites than blacks on welfare and that this figure does not reflect differences in population size. However, Grant is correct that any attempt at a theology of liberation has to take all these

---

22.   Douglas, *The Black Christ* (Maryknoll, NY: Orbis Books, 1994), p. 107.

23.   Douglas, *The Black Christ* (Maryknoll, NY: Orbis Books, 1994), p. 105.

24.   Douglas, *The Black Christ* (Maryknoll, NY: Orbis Books, 1994), p. 108.

25.   Douglas, *The Black Christ* (Maryknoll, NY: Orbis Books, 1994), p. 108.

26.   Jacquelyn Grant, *White Women's Christ, Black Women's Jesus* (Atlanta: Scholars Press, 1989), p. 210.

elements into account. As with all liberation theologies womanists are very careful when it comes to the use of the Bible. It is used but is interpreted from the lives of the people rather than placing layers of dominant interpretation on to their lives. It is through the pages of the Bible and reflection on their lives that womanists have found Jesus, God incarnate, who signifies freedom. This freedom is the kind brought by a political messiah[27] and not simply a spiritual enlightener. Grant sees Christ as black and understands this as a necessary step in understanding what this political liberation would look like. Christ identified as a black woman places the divine among the most deprived and also places a resurrection hope in the midst of despair.

The white Christ cannot give black women a full sense of what liberation could be for them. Grant agrees with many of the arguments put forward by black male theologians, such as James Cone, and civil rights leaders like Malcolm X that it is dangerous for black people to kneel before a white figure of salvation. Of course, for black women kneeling before a white man has added danger. All that is learnt is the 'otherness' of one's own existence, which lends itself to feelings of unworthiness. The process of liberation is not aided by this approach, because the circle leads back to making one vulnerable and prone to victim hood. The white Christ, then, is no liberator for black women.

However, the black female Christ begins to destabilize much of the imagery that has played a negative part in the lives of women. It is possible to begin to understand that the humanity of Jesus was what gave him power and not his maleness alone. This in turn calls for a re-examination of women as representatives of Eve and therefore their lack of ability to represent the divine. In claiming the humanity of Christ as their own black women are becoming subjects in their new and unfolding discourse rather than being objectified in the discourse of others. This new subjectivity does not actually make the womanist position totally exclusivist. In fact, Grant argues that there is an acknowledged universalism at the heart of womanist Christology. The same Christ who works with black women as they fight their tri-dimensional oppression is also in the race struggle with black men, the sexism struggle with all women and the poverty struggle with blacks and whites alike.[28] It is therefore in finding their particularity that black women also find the universally liberating Christ. Although Grant does not explicitly mention it, this understanding of the universality of Christ enables the black/white nature of Christ to be expanded into ethnicity. It has sometimes seemed to observers of

27. Grant, *White Women's Christ, Black Women's Jesus*, p. 215.
28. Grant, *White Women's Christ, Black Women's Jesus*, p. 220.

black theology that black and womanist theologians view the world as simply divided into black and white, underprivilege belonging to black skins and obscene wealth and privilege to white skins. This is, of course, a rather gross generalization and one that was never really a true reflection of the discourse. However, there has not been an explicit acknowledgment of ethnicity. For example, the Irish, who are often very pale skinned, have, and do, suffer under a great deal of ethnic prejudice in Britain. Further, the Cretans under Ottoman rule suffered greatly as do the Tibetans under the Chinese. In other words, 'colour' is not just black and white and prejudice and oppression is not always from the lighter to the darker skins. The next painful step that womanist theology has to take is that of facing the historical reality of black oppression. When blacks sold their black brothers and sisters into slavery, where was the black Christ then? I do not offer this question lightly since it is not meant to undermine the womanist discourse in any way at all. However, just as feminists have had to face the less appealing aspects of women's behaviour, such as their place in slavery, so womanists, if they are to remain honest, have to face the historic and contemporary moments of black oppression. This can only strengthen the discourse through a more nuanced understanding of how Christ the liberator operates in a world that is simply not just black and white.

Womanist theologians are members of a country that is the worst offender against the planet and one that benefits most from the genocidal behaviour of advanced capitalism. The majority of those who suffer globally from this behaviour are people of colour, and so I am not sure that womanists can simply claim a disadvantaged status in the world. (I am not suggesting that any would wish to.) The black Christ moves far beyond the shores of the USA and is asking some searching questions of those who are African Americans. I think this reality calls for another level of reflection, which is not only economic but also racial, and I do not think that affluent African Americans can, on the basis of colour, side with those who suffer. There is a new double jeopardy in which African Americans find themselves, oppressed and oppressor. This need not be a place of despair and womanists could lead the way for the rest of us who have to reflect on this also, for example, Celts who are receiving greater autonomy and have to find just ways of dealing in the world.

Womanist theology destroys any illusion of there being 'good masters', and it exposes the abusive use of the Bible in earlier attempts to create these good masters. What these theologies have done is to turn the use of the Bible into a powerful tool of self-affirmation and prophetic liberation. The God of the Exodus and the black Christ of freedom liberate people from the mind set of oppression and help them to realize that oppression is not the result of cosmic forces or the result of sin. Oppression is always built into a system and as such can always be dismantled. The liberating black Christ calls people to believe that they deserve to be free and that they have the power to achieve that freedom. The black Christ above all else encourages black self-love in a world that encourages self-hatred and self-denial. From this love and self-affirmation comes the power to resist and to work for liberation. From their own recent history womanists can offer ways of empowerment for women of colour who are still in slavery to advanced capitalism throughout the world.

Inculturation and the Christ of Liberation.

Liberation theology in Africa grew alongside moves for independence; moves to break free from European colonization. While the political movements were reinvesting African traditions and institutions with the dignity they deserved, theologians were beginning to ask questions about their religious traditions, which had been suppressed by Christianity. African theologians over the last three decades have engaged with a theology of inculturation; a theology that affirms African culture as a basis for the development of liberation theology. African women theologians have, however, challenged this uncritical adoption of inculturation since not all customs are positive for women in terms of justice and dignity. A theology of liberation cannot be based on cultural practices that are not liberating. This has meant that African women theologians have become engaged with an 'engendered communal theology', a theology that refuses to ignore gender. Hard questions have to be asked and faced if the Christ of liberation is not to be coopted into oppressive cultures. These questions are as much to do with sexuality as with literacy and health care.

The picture is not all gloom, and African theologians, while challenging negative customs, are also reclaiming some of the more positive aspects. These include stories of female deities, leaders and life enhancers. Far from uncritically accepting that Christianity liberated women from the oppressions of African society, the women are examining the negative role of Christianity in women's lives, especially when joined with colonialism. Although such a combination has had a negative influence on all Africans, the way in which it has affected women was distinct. They lost what political and economic power they had and not only suffered under a racist regime but a more patriarchal one. Christianity encouraged women to see the cross as a symbol that helped them bear their suffering rather than resist it. A critique of this approach has not caused women to abandon Christianity altogether but rather to examine the ways in which Christ can liberate them within their culture. African feminist theologians have an immovable belief that Christ is on their side and will help them create just societies. There is then a tension in Christology, since liberation lies both in the help of Christ now and the future just society that will exist. Underpinning this is the knowledge that Jesus is their personal friend who accepts them as they are and wishes to meet their needs in a personal way.[29] This christological development highlights the extent to which women in the African context need such a friend and advocate, one who will touch and heal them both spiritually and physically.

Jesus is also viewed as the one who enfleshes the power of God and is able to share that power with those who follow him.[30] It is the sharing of his power that is particularly relevant for women and other oppressed groups, since this power is shared by all his followers and not just the elite. The power of Jesus is often prophetic, and this means that there are a number of black Messiahs in the independent churches, that is, those who have embodied the prophetic nature of Jesus. These prophetic voices are often raised in relation to social justice issues and so lend a powerful impetus to the struggle for freedom. The prophetic voice, the one that speaks out, is the saving voice for Africa. It is the voice that speaks of the encounter between people and God in the diverse situations of their lives, and in the African context it is the one that demands justice for Africa on the world stage. On a continent that is ravaged by the AIDS virus the Christ of liberation is needed more than ever. The cost in human life does not come alone, it carries with it serious implications for the infrastructure of the continent and this in turn impacts on the living. The prophetic voices, which spread the hope of the liberating Christ, are needed more than ever, but so is aid and cancellation of external debt. These are the demands of the Christ of liberation.

The Christ of liberation takes on many different faces when placed in the lives of women. We see there is a move from the champion of the poor to the advocate of sexual justice in Africa. What feminist theologians have brought to light is that poverty does not come alone, nor is it the only crushing circumstance in life. Women, who are statistically the poorest of the poor, have to engage with many other aspects of their being that crush rather than liberate, not least their colour and gender. The debate has moved on a great deal since Ruether advocated a liberating prophet as that closest to our Jewish roots, yet Christ the liberator continues to shine through the diverse situations of

29. Teresa Hinga, 'Jesus Christ and the Liberation of Women in Africa', in Ursula King, *Feminist Theology from the Third World* (London: SPCK, 1994), pp. 352-57 (266).

30. Hinga, 'Jesus Christ', p. 267.

hardship and oppression. Indeed, we witness a strange phenomenon: as Christ liberates women so they liberate him from the straitjacket of metaphysics and absolutes, which have inhibited incarnation. They appear to birth him once again but this time into a fuller humanity.

Chapter Three

Embodied Christ

Christianity has at its heart the belief that God became incarnate, a belief that places the flesh as the crucial component in the disclosure of the divine: the Word became flesh and dwelt among us. Ironically, then, Christian history displays great ambivalence to the body and at times outright hostility. We have no evidence to suggest that Jesus and his followers were anti-flesh, and certainly the dominant strains within Judaism at the time of Jesus were not fleeing the flesh. Undoubtedly, the influence of Greek metaphysics on the developing Christian movement had a detrimental affect as far as the body was concerned, and the splitting of the person of Jesus into spirit and matter laid the foundations for centuries of body denying and spirit-affirming asceticism.

Women fared badly under this scheme, since according to the great fathers of the church, Augustine and Aquinas, women are mere matter and not disposed to rationality and spirituality in the same way as men. Many of the fathers portrayed women as almost demonic and they saw the act of intercourse as symbolic of the higher spirit getting trapped in matter. Those women who kept themselves chaste and mortified their flesh were considered holy and at times understood to be honorary males.

Christianity, then, has had trouble with embodiment, and so have women. Our bodies have dictated, often brutally, our position in the world from trophy to tart to invisible. Further, medics to psychologists have declared female embodiment problematic and non-normative. Do we see a link! The women's movement, of course, challenged these negative attitudes as well as championing issues connected with the bodies of women, such as abortion, contraception, health issues, conjugal rights and fair wages. Women's experience became the starting point for thinking through many of these issues.

The insights of the women's movement were slow to impact on theology and very slow indeed when it came to matters concerning the female body. However, we now see an explosion of theology addressing issues around incarnation starting from women's experience. In this reclaiming of women's experience as part of an ongoing incarnational revelation, Christ is changing from the strict guardian of improper/weak women into a passionate and embodied embrace.

Among those who envisage an embodied Christ is Elisabeth Moltmann-Wendel. For her the stories about Jesus and women are less androcentrically edited than the rest of the Gospels and she feels that here we see something of the true dynamics of Jesus and so this is a place to start to find Christ. Once we move away from Jesus as the supremely powerful miracle worker we see that the power that makes us whole is our own. Moltmann-Wendell argues that this power is experienced mutually and therefore we do not affect our own salvation in an exclusive sense. She shows how important mutual experience is by illustrating that the stories of women are quite distinct from those of men. The men came to Jesus with questions and discussions while the women came with feeling and seeking to relate.[1] However, by the time of the second generation of Christians Jesus has lost his earthly sensual touching character and 'the Christ' is a set of cerebral beliefs. Moltmann-Wendel illustrates how this process developed with reference to the story of the woman with the haemorrhage. In Mark's tale she touches Jesus, but when the story is retold in Matthew, it is only Jesus' mind that is touched (Mt. 9.21). Moltmann-Wendel sees this as the workings of patriarchy that have already split mind and body, giving higher status to the mind.[2] She shows that the idea of power is already being distorted in the gospels. Jesus exercises his power through loving and relating (Mk 10.45) and the women do the same (Mk 1.31; Mk 15.41), but the men are concerned with who should be first (Mk 10.37). The stories of the crucifixion also highlight the changes taking place. In Mark the word 'theorein' is used to describe what the women were doing at the cross. It means perceiving, understanding and knowing in the same sense as 'knowing the signs' as used in Jn 2.23. It is not an intellectual activity but means that one is totally caught up in and affected by the events. It signals that the women were being wounded by what they were immersed in witnessing. By the time Luke tells the story he uses 'theasthai', which suggests they were simply onlookers.[3] The sense of mutuality in relation is lost by the time the tale is retold by Luke.

Moltmann-Wendel is arguing that there is an alternative tradition in Scripture which has been buried by patriarchy but can be recovered. She

1.   Elisabeth Moltmann-Wendel, *A Land flowing with Milk and Honey* (London: SCM Press, 1986), p. 125.

2.   Moltmann-Wendel, *A Land*, p. 124.

3.   Moltmann-Wendel, *A Land*, p. 134.

suggests that the stories of Jesus and women show a love that transcends class, race, sex and moral value. Discipleship flows from this love and is not an act of obedience but a form of communication that produces community. We read:

> But the God whom Jesus proclaimed is rooted in the matriarchal Sophia tradition. Jesus' way of addressing God as Abba and the sisterly non-patriarchal order which he depicts are in accordance with this picture of God. If the gospels illustrate the disastrous move from mutuality to hierarchical power then the writings of Paul present us' with a piece of male theorising. A personal experience is made the basis for a universal valid theory, his own experience of guilt becomes our own experience of God.[4]

God becomes separated from guilty humanity and Paul's guilt assists him in developing an idea of atonement, which had nothing at all to do with Jesus' death and his ideas about salvation. By doing this Paul helps us to escape the radical nature of the message and avoid the call to be involved. The mutuality and challenge of love are lost. This has serious consequences for everyone but particularly for women. It becomes extremely difficult for women to claim their full humanity and right to divine power within this kind of patriarchal and guilt-ridden Christianity, resting as it does on the fall of humanity from a state of perfection instigated by the actions of a woman.

Moltmann-Wendel is aware of the difficulties but is hopeful women can change the system and humanize the patriarchal God just as Jesus tried to do. The images are there in Scripture, but most of all

> we have the images in us, in our bodies, in our self consciousness. We develop them among us…We are the church and if we reject the pernicious heresy of the separation of the spirit and body…we shall be in the thick of the process which cannot be restrained any longer.[5]

So she is declaring that Jesus encourages us to take our humanity seriously and in so doing transform the world by the sheer outpouring of our dunamis. We can bring God back from the clouds and the impotence that implies and make the Kingdom of Mothers in this world by the radical nature of mutuality, which produces right relation and justice.

By reclaiming Jesus' humanity we also declare our own and emphasize the dignity of being human. The image of Jesus as an extremely powerful miracle worker has meant that we lose sight of our own divine power in relationality and our place in the divine process. Moltmann-Wendel argues that this power in relation is enormously sensuous. People's bodies are touched and engaged

---

4.   Moltmann-Wendel, *A Land*, p. 172.
5.   Moltmann-Wendel, *A Land*, p. 183.

with, anointed, given food and nurtured. She says, 'The word, which became so overpowering above all in the Protestant churches, is only an accompaniment to this experience of the senses'.[6] This is particularly noticeable in encounters with women, while those with men tend to remain wordy and thus their dynamic is restricted. For Moltmann-Wendel there is something about the earthiness and sensuality of Jesus' actions that is essentially Christic. We should then be following the example of Jesus and embracing our bodies and those of others and the planet in a passionate dance of Christic enactment.

Erotic Power and the Life of Christ

Rita Brock and Carter Heyward are the two feminist theologians most associated with the notion of Christ as erotic power. Rita Brock believes that when speaking of Jesus as powerful we have to be quite clear about what type of power we are speaking of; she feels it is erotic power. This leaves us in no doubt about where the source of this power lies; it is not an abstract concept but is deeply embedded in our very being. It does not descend from on high but is part of our nature; it is our innate desire to relate for justice and growth. This kind of power is wild and cannot be controlled, and living at this level saves us from the sterility that comes from living by the head alone. Eros allows us to feel our deepest passions in all areas of life and to reclaim them from the narrow sexual definition that has been used by patriarchy. Christianity has always encouraged agape, which Brock sees as heady and objective and therefore not as something that will change the world. Eros, on the other hand, will engage us and so can change the world. Brock is convinced that erotic power redeems both the world and Christ.

Therefore, our Christology needs to begin in our deepest form of connectedness and our ability to create and sustain relationships; we have to allow ourselves to feel. We have been encouraged to look the wrong way, and this Brock refers to as the broken heart of patriarchy. We have been encouraged to rip ourselves away from what is dear to us: from feeling, the earth, others, ourselves. Brock believes that it is heart that is the original grace and that in exploring the depth of our hearts we find incarnate in ourselves the divine reality of connection. The divinity that we find lies in the heart's fragility; we are vulnerable, and it is this openness to the world that makes us both vulnerable *and* redeemers of the world. We are, as Jesus was, broken-hearted healers. The only way to heal both others and ourselves is in and through our redeeming vulnerability.

6.   Moltmann-Wendel, *A Land*, p. 125.

The major christological implication from this way of thinking is to reject the way Jesus has been portrayed as a static figure who is a victim and who had to be delivered to some outside force and placed in an abstract realm where he dwells in non-present reality as the redeemer. Women have not found the victim role to be redeeming and so question how Jesus could have found it so for himself, let alone for anyone else. Brock is suggesting that in giving back power to Jesus and refusing to see him as the victim, we are also seeing the Christ as an image of shared power that increases in the sharing rather than as a once and for all event in the person of Jesus.

Brock wishes to redeem Christ from being a victim and from being a hero, which is what she says liberation theology does to him. Liberation theology still has the sin salvation model with Jesus in the role of hero for the community if not for the individual. We need no longer see him as the exclusive revelation of God, and then we remove ourselves from the place of simply being acted upon and him from the place of ultimate problem solver.

We should begin to see Christ as larger than the historical Jesus and in that way the Christ becomes more accessible to us. The erotic power of Christ that worked in Jesus becomes the spur for us to go and do likewise, but it is not a guarantee of redemption. Like Moltmann-Wendel, Brock uses the healing stories to illustrate her point, and she suggests that they show how connection was established and how that profound mutuality transformed the situation from one of brokenness to one of wholeness. In demonstrating the effects of erotic power the healing stories show us our own divine power as much as they do Jesus'. Jesus did not explain sickness, he cured it, and we should see this as a normative way for the Christian life. Sickness has all kinds of causes, and in being healers we should also name and cure the causes: pollution, alienation, exploitation, and abuse. Challenging ways of life that reduce individuals and the planet is central to Christianity, which is a religion dedicated to life in abundance. Our political action is then as curative as any laying on of hands. Indeed, it is a community action that aids growth in mutuality unlike 'dispensed healing' which disempowers groups and individuals.

The exorcisms as much as the healings are statements against the societal causes of illness. The biblical picture of exorcisms is not one of personal sin bringing about possession, therefore personal penance is not the way to overcome it. Further, exorcisms are not performed by Jesus because he has the power to forgive but because he has experienced those same demons and so has been empowered by his own experience to release others. The temptation stories show a wounded healer who understands vulnerability and inner oppression. Brock claims the same is true of us: once we name our own demons we release more of our erotic potential and we have the power to help others claim their erotic power. In this way erotic power is not only political but also relational.[7] How intimate this power is and how physically based it is can be seen by Jesus using breath, spittle and blood. Miracles do not require the bestowing of hierarchal power or ritually pure surroundings, they require basic, embodied connection (Mk 6.6). Even the healer needs healing, and Brock uses the anointing of Jesus to illustrate this point.

Brock continues this theme by focusing on the women at the cross who also illustrate the power of heart:

> Heart is our original grace. In exploring the depths of heart we find incarnate in ourselves the divine reality of connection, of love…But its strength lies in fragility. To be born so open to the presence of others in the world gives us the enormous, creative capacity to make life whole. Yet such openness means that the terrifying and destructive factors of life are also taken into the self, a self that then requires loving presence to be restored to grace.[8]

It is in finding our heart that we realize how we have been damaged and our original grace has become distorted. This memory and the anger we should feel at this memory opens us to our deepest passions, and it is here that our erotic power lies, a power that is enhanced by relationship and not by control and dominance. Erotic power is wild, uncontrolled and beautiful. It is this wild heart that saves us from the sterility of living purely in the head. Erotic power and embodied knowing involve subjective engagement of the whole self in relationship.[9] Brock claims that divine reality and redemption are love in all its fullness, an embodied love beating in the heart of a broken-hearted healer. This struggle is the redemptive power of Christ and is no guarantee of anything; there may be no happy endings.

Carter Heyward's starting point for seeking to understand God is that of taking human experience seriously. She says, 'We are, left alone untouched until we choose to take ourselves—our humanity—more seriously than we have taken our God'.[10] Her emphasis is on experiencing God as a living reality and not as a plausible abstract concept. Theology lived by women is not about systems of dogmas, doctrines and categories, but is rather '[a] revelation of a living God whom we believe to be Godself defiant of all static, rigid categories

---

7. Brock, *Journeys by Heart*, p. 82.
8. Brock, *Journeys by Heart*, p. 17.
9. Brock, *Journeys by Heart*, p. 40.
10. Carter Heyward, *The Redemption of God: A Theology of Mutual Relation* (Lanham, MD: University Press of America, 1982).

and concepts'.[11] The traditions have to be tried in relation to women's experience, and if they are crushing and not liberating they have to be discarded.
Indeed, they have to be declared blasphemous and idolatrous because they lie
about the nature of God and limit the unfolding of the Godself. This is not a
task to be done alone but is a relational task. Heyward makes it abundantly
clear how important relating is in the creation of theology in the introduction
to 'Touching our Strength. The Erotic as Power and the Love of God'.[12] Here
she tells us that in order to come to the point of being able to write theology
she had to ground herself, to situate herself in her embodiedness through
touch, smell, taste and memory. Memory of those she had cared for and of the
battles that had been fought and were being fought both personally and
internationally. She had to spend painstaking time and playful time with
friends and she had to make love. All these actions grounded her, embodied
her and placed her in relation. Only then could she reflect theologically.

As we explore Heyward's thought we get a clearer idea of what relating
means. It is the creational/redemptive divine process, ours as well as God's.
She writes:

> In the beginning was God
> In the beginning was the source of all that is
> God yearning
> God moaning
> God labouring
> God giving birth
> God rejoicing
> And God loved what She had made
> And God said
> 'It is good'
> And God knowing that all that is good is shared
> Held the Earth tenderly in Her arms
> God yearned for relationship
> God longed to share the good Earth,
> And humanity was born in the yearning of God
> We were born to share the Earth [13]

Here we see that if God loves us then we are needed, since 'A lover needs
relation—if for no other reason, in order to love'.[14]

11.   Heyward, *The Redemption of God*, p. 12.
12.   Carter Heyward, 'Touching our Strength. The Erotic as Power and the Love of
God', (New York: HarperCollins, 1989).
13.   Heyward, 'Touching our Strength. The Erotic as Power and the Love of God', (New
York: HarperCollins, 1989).
14.   Carter Heyward, *Our Passion for Justice* (Ohio: Pilgrim Press, 1984), pp. 49-50.

God's creative power is the power to love and to be loved. Heyward declares that it was this incarnate, loving, dynamic, relating God that Jesus made visible and that the church lost. She thinks that in the development of Greek Christology the ultimacy of the voluntary character of the divine–human covenant was lost.[15] To preserve the unity of divinity and humanity in Jesus, Chalcedon compromised the possibility of a voluntary union between a human Jesus and the divine God and opted for a hypostatic or essential union of the two natures, the implication being that the possibility of free relation to God was replaced by the idea of inner union, almost an inner compulsion. Heyward says:

> For Jesus history was the realm of righteousness. For Christians earth became a waiting room for some other world where the righteousness achieved by Jesus would be fully revealed. Jews worked for the Messiah, Christians waited for the parousia.[16]

The acceptance of such a doctrine changed the emphasis on justice. Instead of being something people worked for it became something God granted as a gift in the form of natural justice. It was not important to love your neighbour and our world but crucial to love God who was above both.

Heyward suggests that Jesus saw no difference between our love for our God and our love for our neighbour [Mk 12.28-31]. Therefore, we are labouring to create a new life based on mutual love, one in which '[We] are dealing with a real love for man for his own sake and not for the love of God.' [17] There can be no passive observance if we are to be in mutual relation.

Heyward is convinced that this is what the life of Jesus showed us, and she embarks on a task she calls 'imaging Jesus'. Re-imaging may mean letting go of tradition. One such letting go is realizing that Jesus only really matters if he was human and if we view his incarnation as a 'relational experience.'[18] Heyward believes it is a crippling mistake to see Jesus as a divine person 'rather than as a human being who knew and loved God'. It is crippling because it prevents people claiming their own divinity. She does not deny the possibility of incarnation, indeed, if God is a God of relation then incarnation is bound to be not only a possibility but a desirable necessity. She is not devaluing the reality of incarnation but rather exposes the limits of exclusivity. By re-imaging Jesus she also re-images human beings through realizing the amazing power and relation that lies dormant in human nature.

15. Heyward, *The Redemption of God*, p. 7.
16. Heyward, *The Redemption of God*, p. 3.
17. Heyward, *The Redemption of God*, p. 5.
18. Heyward, *The Redemption of God*, p. 16.

Although the Gospels tend to imply Jesus' innate and complete divinity, Luke hints at its growth when he says, 'And Jesus increased in wisdom, in stature and in favour with God and men' (Lk. 2.52). Heyward does not wish to deny God's parenthood of Jesus, but wishes to re-image beyond genetic terms and therefore as the source of power in which Jesus was grounded. Once we really value Jesus' humanity the dualistic gulf between humanity and God is breached. It becomes possible to assert that our own humanity can touch, heal and comfort the world and in so doing strengthen God. At the same time it becomes apparent that a God of love is as dependent on us as we are on her.

Heyward therefore re-images divinity as something we grow towards by choice and activity. This shift requires her to look critically at the notions of authority and power. She is anxious to move away from the idea that authority is something that is exercised over us by God or the state and to come to an understanding of it as self-possessed. Heyward notes that two words are used in the Gospels. One is 'exousia', which denotes power that has been granted, whereas dunamis, which is raw power, innate, spontaneous and often fearful, is not granted but is inborn and is the authority that Jesus claims. This is why Jesus could not answer his interrogators, they were not speaking the same language because they were interested in authority, while he was concerned with power. Nor could he be understood by those who wished to equate authority with religious and civil government. What was new about Jesus was his realization that our dunamis is rooted in God and is the force by which we claim our divinity. By acting with dunamis we, just like Jesus, act from both our human and divine elements. We can overcome the suspicion of human power and initiative placed in our religious understanding by the story of Eve and her actions in Eden. Of course, we have to re-image the kingdom as a place where the lion lies down with the lamb and the tools of destruction are changed into instruments of creativity. When humans dare to acknowledge their divine nature through dunamis, this is the kind of kingdom that is imaginable and must be made incarnate through radical love.

Radical love incarnates the kingdom because intimacy is the deepest quality of relation. Heyward says that to be intimate is to be assured that we are known in such a way that the mutuality of our relation is real, creative and cooperative. It is possible to see Jesus' ministry as based on intimacy since he knew people intuitively, insightfully and spontaneously. Heyward's re-imaging makes it clear that Jesus does not have exclusive rights to dunamis. Indeed, he facilitates our knowing and claiming of God as dunamis through relation. He reveals to us 'the possibility of our own godding.'[19] Of course, time and again people reject

19. Heyward, *The Redemption of God*, p. 31.

this and cling to conformity, and Jesus points out, 'You put aside the commandment of God to cling to human traditions' (Mk 7.8). In his own lifetime this rejection led to Jesus' crucifixion and led to the death of God, not because Jesus was exclusively God but because humanity rejected the possibility of its own dunamis. Heyward says the crucifixion signals 'the extent to which human beings will go to avoid our own relational possibilities.'[20] I believe there is a further denial of Jesus today by Christians who insist on his otherworldly sonship and divinity and in the name of this exclusivity condemn and marginalize people. I would suggest that the extent to which we claim exclusive and remote divinity for Jesus is the extent to which we show our lack of faith and commit idolatry through turning Jesus into everything that he stood against, in other words, into a false God.

Heyward also questions the wisdom of referring only to the last few days of Jesus' life as his Passion. She thinks it is necessary to broaden the term and realize that mutual relation involves one in living passionately at all times and in all areas of one's life. She argues that if there is power in relation then there is pain in lack of relation.[21] Jesus, while experiencing God so intimately, could not avoid the pain of realizing that God was denied and broken when relational power was broken. Jesus would not have to go beyond himself to see that he too doubted and therefore damaged this power (Mk 15.34). Heyward sees Jesus' death as releasing people not because it was good, but because he refused to flee from it, thus showing how committed he was to ongoing passionate relationality. We should be angry about injustice and suffering and not accept it as a blessing. Hard as it is for women and other marginalized people to do, we should view anger positively and allow ourselves to experience it; Jesus did (Mk 9.19; 10.14; 11.15-19; 12.38-40; 14.6). If we look at his anger we find it is usually directed at injustice, non-relationality and misuse of humanity. If we get angry enough and keep our courage, perhaps we too can witness the reality of a new way, a kingdom on earth. Heyward does not go into great detail about the resurrection but she does say that, whatever it was, it did not remove or lessen the injustice of Jesus' death. She says it is possible to re-image it as a seed planted in the soil of Jesus' decomposition and harvested forever in his friends' subsequent refusals to give up intimacy and immediacy with God. In this way Christianity is a resurrection faith as long as those who follow it preserve intimacy, power in relation and passion.

Heyward's Christ is one who meets us where we are between the 'yet' and the 'not yet' and impresses upon us not so much the nature of the Christ but

20. Heyward, *The Redemption of God*, p. 47.
21. Heyward, *The Redemption of God*, p. 48.

the meaning of who we are.[22] Therefore, the Christ is a friend who empowers but not a God who will manipulate. In this way, 'God's incarnations are as many and varied as the persons who are driven by the power in relation to touch and be touched by sisters and brothers'.[23] Most of all Heyward's Christology is fully embodied, sensuous and erotic, seeking vulnerable commitment, alive with expectancy and power.

Heyward is only too well aware that traditional Christianity will have difficulty accepting such an experientially based Christology, based as it is in lesbian embodiment. It is, however, her lesbianism that plays a large part in her christological explorations, as it is the ground of her experience of mutuality and her most embodied reality. Indeed, she has since argued that the kind of mutuality she is expounding is most easily found between women. The power dynamics of gender do not make it an easy matter for men and women to find mutual empowerment in their most intimate acts. However, like Brock she declares that the resurrection highlights how the power of connectedness can live on in others despite Jesus' physical absence. The concept of resurrection is a testimony to the healing power inherent in the world, and this includes the healing of the rupture in gender power relations set in place by patriarchy.

This Is my Body; This Is my Blood

Women's embodiment played no part in the theology of the early fathers of liberation theology. An area left almost untouched by the male Christ of liberation in Latin America is that of reproductive rights. No connection was made between the poverty of women and their reproductive rights. Feminist theologians in Latin America and Asia graphically illustrate the way in which liberation theology left solely in the hands of men has a partial agenda. Certainly, it is true that women suffer terribly through poverty, but this raises related issues for them that have been overlooked by the fathers of liberation theology. For example, there is also a striking silence on domestic violence and back street abortions, which is perhaps a good thing, since most liberation theologians when dealing with these issues take a decidedly Vatican line. It has to be acknowledged that not many of the women are vocal on these matters either, Ivone Gebara being one of the few to speak in favour of legalizing abortion. Her view is based on the realization that women will always have to resort to abortion. There are between 36 and 53 million abortions a year

22. Heyward, *The Redemption of God*, p. 54.
23. Heyward, *The Redemption of God*, p. 163.

worldwide, of which 30–50 per cent are illegal. Gebara is realistic and would rather that women had safe choices.

The issue of reproductive rights in Latin America is not as straightforward as in Europe, due to what has been called contraceptive imperialism. There has historically been interference in governmental population policies by multinational companies and development agencies. This has ranged from pressure for widespread sterilization to flooding the countries with hormonal contraceptives that have not been properly tested. While feminists are keen to resist this kind of intervention, they are also keen to give women control over their own bodies, viewing this as fundamental in talk of liberation.

Victory of a kind was won at the Cairo International Conference on Population and Development in 1994. It was at this conference that the Vatican made its famous and staggering alliance with Muslim fundamentalists in order to prevent the inclusion of reproductive rights and abortion in the final conference document. Women's organizations from North and South were successful in preventing this unholy alliance achieving its aims. It was perhaps a first, but significant, move towards women being placed at the centre of debates about reproductive rights and abortion.

It would be too easy to say that the reason such questions have not been addressed by the male liberating Christ is because of the machismo in Latin American countries. This is in part true as it makes women invisible. However, a celibate male clergy, modelling the life of Christ, also adds to the silence because they simply do not see the problem. The Christ of liberation has not been released quite enough from the straitjacket of dualistic metaphysics despite his new 'historic look'. It is this focus on a Christ who is in some way complete, whole and celibate that relegates all questions to do with sexual ethics to the margins. So Christ the liberator does not go quite far enough for some women in Latin America

Feminist theologians, however, are not afraid to deal with the fleshy reality of Jesus and connect it with their own lives. Maria Clara Bingemer argues that women's bodies are eucharistic.[24] She understands the eucharist to refer to the incarnation, death and resurrection of Christ and declares that women 'possess in their bodiliness the physical possibility of performing the divine eucharistic action. In the whole process of gestation, childbirth, protection and nourishing of a new life, the sacrament of the eucharist, the divine act, happens anew'.[25]

24. Heyward, *The Redemption of God*, p. 164.

25. Maria Clara Bingemar, 'Women in the Future of the Theology of Liberation', in Ursula King (ed.), *Feminist Theology from the Third World* (London: SPCK, 1994).

What exactly is she saying? Are women the Christ of the eucharist? What difference, if any, does she see between the divine action of the eucharist and the divine creative action of women? It appears there is no difference. She extends the divinely creative actions of women's bodies beyond that of giving birth to toiling in the fields and factories in order to provide life for others. Most of all the bodies of women in Latin America are placed in the struggle for liberation. She says, 'Woman's body, eucharistically given to the struggle for liberation, is really and physically distributed, eaten and drunk by those who will—as men and women of tomorrow—continue the same struggle'.[26]

We almost hear the words 'take eat this is my body' as we picture women standing against the many faces of oppression that afflict them. Bingemer moves the christological debate on many steps when she equates the bodies of women with the eucharistic body of Christ, not least because these are real bodies that experience the pleasures and pains of being fully incarnate. These women laugh, cry, love, hate, make love, are raped or beaten, are violated by the system and often abuse others. Can these bodies really be the body of Christ in the eucharistic sense? A resounding 'yes' is the answer. Bingemer is not referring to women being the body of Christ in the community sense of church but rather in their own embodied existence, in both the good and the bad. Their embodied struggle is the essence of Christ. This places a new slant on Jesus as 'companero', or fellow revolutionary. He has been understood almost as the 'ultimate revolutionary' This is not, however, the way in which some feminists wish to see him. His part in their struggle is far more intimate, he is not their leader, he is the struggle, he is their embodiment within it. What is raised here, in a striking way, is the notion that incarnation and perfection do not sit easily together. The Christ of otherworldly, yet enfleshed, perfection is taken to task and found lacking. What good is such a Christ to women whose compromised flesh needs liberation?

Gabriele Dietrich[27] goes further and actually suggests a female image of Christ, in this way truly embedding Christ in the struggle for liberation but this time in the Indian context. She makes a powerful connection between the salvific blood of Jesus on the cross and women's menstrual blood. She claims that women's blood cries out, placing in front of us the many injustices that the female body suffers. She writes:

> I am a woman
> and the blood
> of my sacrifices

26. Bingemar, 'Women in the Future', p. 317.
27. Bingemer, 'Women in the Future', p. 317.

cries out to the sky
which you call heaven.[28]

It cries out in rage against abuse, forced abortion, colonization of the womb by clerics and the denial of women's embodied power. Dietrich dwells on the loss in this kind of bloodshed and reminds us that women's blood has always been shed, but for life, since eternity. This shedding is truly salvific unlike the glorification of male blood in the hands of priests. The worship of Christ's blood, shed as it was through torture and public execution, has crippled women through guilt and unworthiness. What Bingemer and Dietrich enable women to do is honour their own natural blood shedding and rage against the way in which they have been bled of self-respect and life itself by a patriarchal system fetishistically worshipping the blood of a dead man. There is a call here for life, a call to turn from morbid necrophilia to an embrace of strong, competent, life-giving women; a call to honour the womb and not manipulate it to serve patriarchal power.

Dietrich challenges the church that honours the womb for procreation but uses it symbolically to ban women from full participation in the life of the church. We should realize that Jesus and women are joined through the shedding of life-giving blood. Both, it could be argued, struggle to be creative in a world that finds it easier to abuse than to love. Indeed, both also carry the pain of knowing that what they love could so easily be destroyed. The blood of women, then, menstrual and otherwise, is a sign of eucharistic community, understood as centred commitment and passionate action.

Other Indian women are developing the Hindu concept of Shakti, which is the underlying power of the cosmos, the one who represents the primal creative energy and are reclaiming their own power. It is this concept that illustrates the relatedness of humans and nature since it throbs in both. Ironically, this all-powerful and creative force, said to be present in women and to represent the true essence of Indian womanhood, is not respected in society at large. If it were the position of women in Indian society would be better. Aruna Gnanadason [29] argues that this power has been submerged under patriarchal interpretations of religion as well as development models that emerge from the west. She believes that the future hope for the whole of creation lies in the reawakening of women's Shakti; the Great Mother Goddess has to stir in the souls of women once more if the world is to survive and flourish.

Many Indian women are experiencing the reawakening of this spiritual path

---

28. Gabriele Dietrich quoted in Chung Hyun Kyung, *Struggle to Be the Sun Again* (London: SCM Press, 1990), pp. 66-70.

29. Chung, *Struggle*, p. 66-70.

and it makes them profoundly suspicious of traditional religion. They are questioning the status that religion has ascribed to women and are seeking ways to break out from the straitjacket of convention. This is a community-based undertaking, since Indian women have no desire to make the same mistake of overt individualism that many western feminists made. Rather they wish to affirm the dignity and uniqueness of individuals as part of a community. In turn these communities and the individuals that comprise them, are actively involved in the critique of life-denying structures within their society. At a time when fundamentalism seems to be on the increase in all parts of the world, the women of India are demonstrating the strengths of pluralism. The fundamentalist surge has resulted in many restrictions placed on women, and so the celebration of womanhood that is part of the re-emergence of Shakti is vitally important if women are to retain any sense of self. As the restrictions placed upon them are embodied, physical, so Indian women need to embody their challenge. This is the power of Shakti in the lives of many Indian women today.

Christ in Latin America and Asia is truly incarnate and alive through women's experience. This Christ not only re-empowers the bodies of women but is active through the ancient traditions in India to remind patriarchy that primal, creative energy emanates from the female divine and draws all together in embodied creativity to push against oppression. In addition this energy roots women in the body of the great mother—the earth. The bodies of women and that of nature learn to dance their embodied power together.

Incarnate in a Bleeding Continent.

Feminist theologians in Africa are aware that the challenge they bring is one that will have deep significance for the future. Therese Souga sees the challenge that women bring as following the example of women, mostly unnamed, in the Gospels. The Syro-Phoenician woman (Mt. 15.21-28) or the woman with the haemorrhage (Mt. 9.18-22) are very embodied examples of how ill-conceived stereotypes of women, even those held by Jesus himself, have to be faced, challenged and overcome. These women were not only persistent but they questioned how they were viewed by society and made known their own reality. Souga believes that African women are challenging the negative stereotypes of them that persist in the African church in the same way that these foremothers in faith did.[30] She concludes that they too will receive the healing

---

30.   Aruna Gnanadason, 'Women and Spirituality in Asia', in Ursula King (ed.), *Feminist Theology from the Third World* (London: SPCK, 1994), pp. 352-53.

that these women demanded. It is, however, a healing that is dispensed by Jesus, and she does not lay emphasis on the role of the women in bringing about their healing except through their persistence. With western eyes it would seem that more could be made of the Christ-like actions of the gospel women themselves and not just of their challenge of the oppressive systems that kept them restricted and prevented their access to healing.

Nonetheless these foremothers are seen as models for the active participation of African women in overcoming their cultural oppression. Feminist theologians in Africa are daring to break the taboos around the issues of sexuality, a brave act in a culture that would remove women from that discourse altogether. It is, however, a much needed courage on a continent ravaged by AIDS. While this would appear at first glance to make the Christ of Africa one of suffering, there is also an element of self-determination. Women are not dealing with this issue in isolation. It is just one of an array of issues, such as polygamy, clitoridectomy, child marriage, prostitution and barrenness, that affect women and impact on lives with devastating consequences. In arguing for the dignity of women and the ability to choose, feminist theologians in Africa are declaring a Christ who sees them as full human beings; as persons capable of flourishing beyond the strict and disabling constraints of patriarchy as found on their continent. By asserting this through issues related to female embodiment, feminist theologians are moving the debate away from the suffering Christ and beyond the liberating prophet. This is a Christ who stands with women as they challenge the most debilitating aspects of their culture and demand justice for their bodies in a culture that has learnt to abuse them.

For African women 'real Christology' is performed each day as they struggle against the multifaceted oppressions that face them. This struggle is fuelled by an unshakeable belief that Jesus and his followers change history. This is the Christ that will shake the west much more than Constantine's conquering hero Christ, and the shaking will come from the cry for justice issuing from the bodies of our sisters on the African continent. They are heavily burdened and they continue to embody Christic action by finding life-giving circumstances for their children.

Indecent and Oh So Queer Christ

Marcella Althaus-Reid proposes an indecent theology that she develops from her background in Argentina where women were defined through the concept of decency, a concept that entered Latin America with the Conquistadors:

> It is closely related to the objectification of women as property through the institution of colonial marriage, the exaltation of reproduction amongst the white, foreign elite under judicial superstructure committed to inheritance laws, and also to the confinement of women in certain legal although the word used is 'decent' physical, emotional and economic spaces.[31]

Women on the margins of this tightly regulated society rebelled against decency either through choice or necessity, that is, the categories did not fit their lived experience. They were unable to be defined and contained by imperial inventions, and in their 'indecency' found new life-giving ways. Women who worked in factories or took part in revolutionary struggle were defined as indecent and were seen as sexually available. Through the embodiment of these women Christ is indecent, the one who expands the edges of categories and seeks life.

Althaus-Reid says:

> The fact is that the Christological process starts not with the first meetings of church councils but with the construction of the Christ, the Messiah, a process that depends on the interrelationality between a man called Jesus and a community of women, men and children.[32]

For this reason Althaus-Reid engages with Coya women, those who wear no underwear, carry their children on their backs and let their sexual smells blend with their surroundings as they work and pray. The bodies of these women are starting points for Christology just as the body of Jesus was. Indeed, as they are the poorest women, liberation theology is bound to start with them.

Althaus-Reid critiques the way in which male liberation theologians have almost romanticized christological images. We have the Christ who embraces the poor and Christ the Peruvian peasant on the cross. For Althaus-Reid this is not even half the story, as it does not shift the Christological core far enough. If the truly poor are to be embraced then we should be imaging Christ as a young girl prostituted by two men in a public toilet in Buenos Aires.[33] This is too strong an image for many liberation theologians, but it is the very stuff of

31. Therese Souga, 'The Christ Event from the Viewpoint of African Women', in Virginia Fabella and Mercy Amba Oduyoye (eds.), *With Passion and Compassion* (Maryknoll, NY: Orbis Books, 1994), pp. 131-38 (250).

32. Marcella Althaus-Reid, 'The Indecency of Her Teaching: Notes for a Cureb Teaching of Feminist Theology in Europe', in Elisabeth Schüssler-Fiorenza and Shawn Copeland (eds.), *Feminist Theology in Different Contexts* (London: SCM Press, 1996), pp. 133-40 (136).

33. Marcella Althaus-Reid, 'On Wearing Skirts without Underwear: Indecent Theology Challenging the Liberation Theology of the Pueblo. Poor Women Contesting Christ', *Feminist Theology* 20 (Sheffield: Sheffield Academic Press, 1999), pp. 39-51.

indecent theology, as it tells the truth about women's lives. Althaus-Reid argues that liberation theology has fought for equality but not for diversity, and therefore many women have been left out of the process since, in a strange way, only the 'decent' are worthy of equality. She argues that a new understanding of Christ is needed, one that moves away from the Christ as the fetish of Christianity and the patriarchal discourse that underpins it. We need to move Christ away from the heterosexual, masculinist model that speaks about power relations in the public and private sphere as much as it does about sexuality.

By challenging the gendered construction of Christ we are also challenging the power hierarchy and releasing Christ into a freer and more empowering relationality. By telling indecent sexual stories, those that are the reality of people's lives, we destabilize normative rules that cripple people. This is, then, a Christic act.

Althaus-Reid argues that the image of Christ we have offers women into ritual prostitution, if we understand prostitution as a lack of options: 'The scriptures portray what I call the ritual prostitution of women in the sense that women are presented as emotional and economic sustainers of religion without challenging structurally the epistemological order of which that ritual prostitution belongs'.[34] Christ does not change this for women and so some rethinking is necessary.

Althaus-Reid offers a very challenging image of Christ as Xena, warrior princess. A leather woman hanging on a cross, declaring love into eternity for the woman she loves. This is a queer Christ indeed, one that challenges traditional images on many levels. She is not passive, she is in leather and she is a dyke. She is courageous and transgressive just as Jesus of Nazareth was; so is she a Christ? Certainly she is, because she destabilizes the neat patriarchal hierarchy, which rests on Christ the celibate heterosexual. She is the sort of Christ that women need, one who will free them from preconceptions and the death of stereotypes.

This Christ is transgressive and refuses to 'play it straight'; that is Christ becomes one who acts beyond boundaries. By challenging the narrow boundaries of society this Christ increases the redemptive space and allows a new community to flourish. A community that embodies resistance to the worst excesses of a patriarchal world. The transgressive Christ is also an ethical Christ, one who places our potential for pleasure at the heart of a demand for justice. An ethic of self sacrifice is replaced by one of well-being and pleasure;

34. Althaus-Reid, 'On Wearing Skirts', p. 41.

this is not a purely private matter but one that calls to just action world trade as much as sexual intimacy. Bodies, as much as souls, are called to flourish and a pleasure ethic is our yardstick in this justice seeking.[35]

The embodied Christ is emerging in many forms, and in each incarnation issues are addressed and the creative/redemptive space expanded. There is much here to outrage and to shock, and that is because we have never been allowed to hear each other's stories and have always imagined that Christ, the Word made flesh, is disembodied. The Christ who was made manifest in the life of Jesus was also shocking and subversive, and many of the taboos of his day were transgressed in order that a fuller picture of the glory of God could be seen. The kingdom that Jesus strove for was not a walled-in paradise of like-minded and socially cloned individuals, it extended justice and dignity to all, even the outcasts.

The embodied Christ is going to offer many challenges in this new century because it is set to move far beyond the 'acceptable' issues to do with women's bodies. This Christ is on the move back to where Jesus was most content, among those on the edges of society, and it was here that redemption and the grains of the kingdom were demonstrated to have root. Women's bodies, which have been seen as so scandalous through Christian centuries, are preparing to be indecent on their own terms and in so doing to expand Christic potential and redemptive possibility.

35. Althaus-Reid, 'On Wearing Skirts', p. 47.

Chapter Four

Ecological Christ

An incarnational religion must pay attention to the whole of the created order and the very fibres of the universe itself. Unfortunately this has not always been the way in which Christianity has seen things, preferring to prioritize the experience of men (I make deliberate use of the word) above all else. The origins of this arrogance lie in the interpretations of the Eden myth where the disembodied word of God commanded that the world be brought into being out of nothingness with a hierarchy of creation set in place ending with humans (Gen. 1.27), man (Gen. 2.7) or woman (Gen. 2.22). As the crown of creation the humans are given the task of subduing (Heb. Kabas, 'stamp down') and dominating (Heb. Rada, 'trampling') the world (Gen. 1.28) which is signalled by the power of naming (Gen. 2.19). While man is busy dominating his surroundings, the woman is busy exploring and gaining 'hands on' experience of their environment. She communes with other parts of the created order, seeing them as equal and wishing to gain as much knowledge as possible. We are told that the result was that the Fall of Man occurred. While closer examination reveals a rather different interpretation, this version illustrates the point that interpretation is all.

There is an increasing body of work such as Westermann (1974), Stone (1982) and Long (1991) that suggests that the Genesis story is male polemic against a much older and more ecologically sound goddess culture. The Babylonian texts, that form the background for the Genesis myth are more honest in stating their intentions. They clearly illustrate how the mother goddess is challenged and defeated. The Genesis myth does not declare its intention so openly but all the signs are there. All that was valued and honoured in the goddess culture is cast down and made suspect at best, or the root of all evil, at worst. In the patriarchal myth, women, nature, the wise serpent and the procreative process itself are seen as suspect. Further, woman brought sin into the world, which would ultimately require the death of the only son of God.

None other than Calvin reminded us that the cross on Calvary was planted in Eden. The doctrines of traditional Christian theology read more like cosmic sado-masochism than empowered mutual relation.

Ruether was among the first to highlight the connection between women and nature and the downward spiralling of both in the Christian Scriptures . She believes it takes place on two levels, the cultural-symbolic and the socio-economic. The former has been explored by feminist scholars from many disciplines, who illustrate how, with the definition of culture by males, women are left no other identification than with nature, which is inferior.[1] No one can be sure how this arose but speculation suggests that it may have had its roots in child-bearing and the activities connected with it, such as providing food. Men were less engaged in this work on a daily basis and so had time for 'bigger' tasks carried out less frequently, which also allowed them to decide societal matters.

Ruether argues that the shift to plough agriculture further denigrated women, who continued with food-providing in a more intimate way. Men became interested in owning land, and this also made them concerned about patrilineal descent, which was a shift from matrilineal. In the world of the Hebrew scriptures there is another massive shift when God becomes imaged as male and transcendent. Once Greek metaphysics are added to this mix we have an earth-and-woman denying agenda. This is what we find in the fathers, where women and nature are lumped together as things that the Christian man must rise above. This legacy has been conveyed to us through the centuries and neither the Enlightenment nor the scientific revolution has done much to dislodge the hierarchical thinking.

Our industrial, scientific world has widened the gap between rich and poor, and women bear the brunt of this since they, and the children who depend on them, make up the greatest number of the poor. The cost to nature of this industrial madness is well documented. Worldwide women are labouring under the worst excesses of rampant capitalism, providing health care, education and general care taking to those disaffected by the system. We see then that the relationship between women and nature is still one that signals denigration for both. The plight of one directly affects the plight of the other. Ecofeminism is therefore an important corrective to Christian theology, which has made the male condition central to all questions concerning culture and production.

1.   Sherry Ortner, 'Is Female to Male as Nature Is to Culture?', in Michelle Zimbalist Rosaldo and Louise Lamphere (eds.), *Woman, Culture and Society* (Stanford: Stanford University Press, 1974), pp. 67-87.

The question is whether the global system that has sprung from such thinking can, through a focus on women and nature, be changed. What is needed is a realistic approach that moves away from romantic notions about women and nature and as far away as possible from the destructive influences of dualistic metaphysics and the illusory opposites it creates. Such a conversion is needed if we are to find ways of being inclusive enough to make survival more than a mere hope.

We are facing global crisis not because the earth is dysfunctional and is no longer able to sustain itself but because of the way in which humans approach it and the demands they make of it. This means that we have to accept responsibility for change rather than project inadequacies on to the earth. Further, we have to be mindful of the way in which we attempt to bring about change. It is often thought that the needs of those in the Third World are served through development programmes. However, the work of Shiva and others clearly shows that this is yet another advanced capitalist myth that serves the developed world more than the 'developing world'. While development programmes have created new forms of affluence, they have done so at great expense to the already dispossessed. Focusing on the plight of women, Shiva shows how development has become the problem it was attempting to alleviate. Economic growth has become a new form of colonialism that drains the resources of those who are most in need of them. For example, the expansion of cash crops has actually dispossessed women even further, as it has removed them from a means of production, that of growing food, and has left them with fewer resources to feed their children.

Shiva makes the point that there is now a crisis of survival brought about by development programmes that are patriarchal projects springing from western capitalism. These projects do not fit well with another way of life, nor do they respect the difference. Productivity for survival is a very different matter than productivity to satisfy the capitalist market. Most women in India are poor, and they work daily in the production of survival, yet 'women and nature working to produce and reproduce life are declared "unproductive"'.[2] When control and profit take the upper hand, women and nature become linked in a downward spiral. Shiva declares that the revolution lies in maintaining that the connection between women and the earth has always been in order to enhance life, both of people and the earth itself. It is therefore important that this connection should be given more respect.

Although women are themselves victims of the degeneration of the envi-

2.   Shiva quoted in Rosemary Ruether, *Women Healing Earth* (London: SCM Press, 1996), p. 67.

ronment, they are also active in movements to protect it from the onslaughts of 'development.' Many have developed their own cooperatives in the hope of opting out of mainline development programmes. Although the women become more disempowered by the development programmes, they are still expected to provide for their children by finding fuel and water. Even though there are always children there are not always resources. Women are therefore held hostage to their families and to survival.

Women who challenge the understanding of resources as merely profit are challenging global capitalism at its heart. This is a system that has abused women, men and nature in its relentless pursuit of obscenely large profit margins. This is not an uncritical Marxist critique of the capitalist order but rather a suggestion that capital for its own sake has brought us to the point of extinction. It seems that modes of production should be both person and planet friendly and that capital should serve all people rather than just a few while the rest are faceless servants of its production. The Christ of liberation emerging from the experience of women in connection with nature demands that there is a major paradigm shift away from domination and towards a more mutual and empowering way of production. We desperately need new models of Christ with which to address the crisis in ecology.

Epiphanic, Organic Christ

Ecofeminism is a very important aspect of Asian theology, and of course has christological implications. Kwok Pui-Lan is one of the few Asian theologians explicitly to tackle the implications of ecology for Christology. [3] She is keen to show that she does not place ecology and Christology together because she is over-focused on Christ, but because she believes that the west has been too anthropocentric. [4] This is a fault that arises from the way in which Christ has been envisaged. Within the traditional view God sent his son to live on earth and save us all from sin and grant us life after death. The hidden message is that the natural processes of birth have to be overridden in order that this divine human may be saved from the stain involved in the natural way of things. Further, we can be saved from the natural processes of decay.

Kwok argues that this does not have to be the case, because there is enough biblical evidence to create 'an organic model' of Christ. He calls himself the vine and the disciples the branches, while the breaking of bread together is also

---

3.   Kwok Pui-Lan, 'Ecology and Christology', in *Feminist Theology* 15 (Sheffield: Shef-field Academic Press, 1997), pp. 113-25.

4.   Kwok, 'Ecology and Christology', p. 116.

an organic paradigm. [5] Kwok claims that an organic model of Christ makes plain the interrelatedness of humans and the cosmos. Further, if Jesus is understood as the conveyor of wisdom, as some western feminist theologians would wish, then from an Asian point of view much of that wisdom would be to do with the earth and the way it offers many challenges to the human race. Christ as wisdom, in the Asian understanding, sets a direct challenge to us to find ways to preserve and honour nature. Far from running from the evils that may be awaiting us in nature we should embrace it in loving and courageous solidarity.

This imaging of Christ allows us to move away from colonialism and anthropocentrism towards a more globally empowering sense of the divine. It could, however, be argued that Kwok is perilously close to the idea of the cosmic Christ that was in truth no more than a religious colonization. However, the plurality of her background makes one suspect that this is not her intention at all. What she is doing is adding her own cultural awareness to largely western pictures and changing the vista dramatically. Christ is understood in and through the very stuff that Christians have been so encouraged to flee from. This leads Kwok to question the notion of the once and for all revelation of Christ. He (Christ) is rather 'epiphanic', which means that he is not one but many and that everyone has the potential to attain the status that Jesus attained. This, of course, requires us to give up any dualistic thinking. [6] We are no longer separated from Christ by Greek metaphysics, rather the prototype that Jesus offers points us to the awesome reality that God is among us, in humans and in nature.

This 'Emmanuel' is made manifest when we act for the poor and the marginalized, when we stand against oppression and when we joyfully celebrate life and evoke the power of the divine. These ways of being are not restricted to our interaction with others, they also extend to nature and the cosmos itself. We could argue that the planet is being impoverished daily, placed in slavery to our needs while being neglected and abused. The planet then becomes one of the poor and marginalized that liberation theologians have always sided with in a struggle for justice.

The African search for a holistic Christology throws up a Christ, who is cosmological, who is embedded in a search for justice. Anne Nasimiyu-Wasike images Jesus as the cosmological liberator,[7] the one who hears the groaning of

5.   Kwok, 'Ecology and Christology', p. 121.

6.   Kwok, 'Ecology and Christology', p. 124.

7.   Anne Nasimuyu-Wasike, *An African Woman's Experience in Liberation Theology: An Introductory Reader* (ed. Curt Codorette *et al.*; Maryknoll, NY: Orbis Books, 1992), p. 101.

nature, heals the pain and overcomes the exploitation. Jesus, who calmed the storms in his own day, can overcome the droughts, floods and famines that are killing Africans today. Christ is the one who can restore balance to nature and in this way help the liberation of people. This is a very important element in the christological debate that has been overlooked for centuries by those who have been more comfortable with understanding universal balance as meaning that dominant values will prevail. The point that Nasimiyu-Wasike highlights is a crucial one, which is that liberation has food as its basic component. People have to be in control of their own sustenance, and they must not be dependent for the very basics in life if they are to be seen as truly free. Africa tells a scandalous tale of western intervention that has played a major part in the increase of drought and famine and the increased inability of Africans to cope with it. The colonizer 'knew best' about ways of farming, grazing and crop rotation. Added to this the masters required that resources be used to sustain their wealth and not the population's survival. This combination of arrogance and greed has contributed in great measure to the ruination of many African economies. Much of the land is ruined and many traditional, holistic ways of coping with the environment have been lost or are no longer up to the new tasks. Of course, there are still colonial demands placed on Africa and her people in the name of national debt. A cosmological Christology calls multi-national companies to account and poses serious environmental questions. This Christ requires a major change in both economy and the way in which industry operates and pollutes the cosmos. Africa, along with so many other countries, can no longer be used as a breeding ground for western luxuries. Instead the west should provide aid were needed as compensation for centuries of abuse and should stay out of African politics.

The Cosmic Christ and Other Friends

Anne Primavesi encourages us to relate to things as though they were sacred in themselves and notes that hierarchy is not the only way to ensure against anarchy.[8] She advocates ecological community. This is a concept fuelled by the notions of both the cosmic Christ and process thought. The cosmic Christ highlights the reality that unless all the created order is saved then nothing can be. This places ecology right at the centre of Christian concerns and not as a marginal question to get round to when the important business of individual salvation has been dealt with. No such division can be made, because 'all

---

8.   Anne Primavesi, *From Apocalypse to Genesis: Ecology, Feminism and Christianity* (Tunbridge Wells: Burns & Oates, 1991), p. 151.

creation is simultaneously being loved and created by God or else none of it is'.[9] We have to view the world differently if we take her seriously, she is no longer just as a commodity. By placing Christ in the world in this way we are able to look around and not just upwards in order to see the mystery present in all creation. Primavesi argues that seeing Christ in creation cannot just remain at the mystical level but has to lead to political action. Contemplating the suffering Christ in a world that is drowning in its own waste is not what is required of a Christian; instead, we have to be committed to policies and praxis that clear up the waste and honour the planet.

Primavesi outlines how traditional Christology has created a lack of ecological awareness. By placing Christ outside the created order and theologizing about heaven and the end of time, Christians have often set their face to fleeing the earth rather than engaging with it. By focusing on the cosmic Christ, a very welcome change in emphasis is introduced to the debate. However, this does not go far enough. Why are Christians unable to value the world in itself? Why does it somehow have to be seen as working towards a larger androcentric plan? Halkes is one of the few who openly acknowledges that the created order has its own value system that is not in any way related to ours and may not even be in our interests.[10] She claims this is still a Christian position and is wholly consistent with a feminist acceptance of difference and diversity. The earth may indeed have its own value system, and is quite able to exist without us and not in our interests, and yet still be enlivened by that which we call the divine. Surely it is time for cooperation with the cosmos based on its own integrity rather than our patriarchal value system and the innate destructiveness of androcentric thinking. It seems time to give up our desire for control, embrace our fear of smallness and expand our vision.

Embodied Ecology

McFague[11] attempts to expand our vision by placing both the body and the planet in intimate relation with each other and the divine. The trinity she creates in so doing leaves out the person of Jesus but it could be argued it is still Christic. She advocates a body-based approach, because she feels that we should see trees and planets as bodies. This will enable us to connect in an intimate way with the world. It could open the way to overcoming the

---

9. Primavesi, *From Apocalypse to Genesis*, p. 151.

10. Halkes, *New Creation in Christian Feminism and the Renewal of the Earth* (London: SPCK, 1991), p. 93.

11. Sally McFague, *The Body of God: An Ecological Theology* (London: SCM Press, 1993).

subject/object dualism that has enabled us to exploit the world. This will mean that we stop seeing ourselves as spirits in a material world and instead understand that we are spirited bodies among spirited bodies.[12]

McFague places the emphasis on matter, on bodies, because of her understanding of the way the universe itself evolved and functions. It took one very hot piece of matter approximately one-millionth of a gram in weight to spawn billions of galaxies, planets and stars. For McFague this underpins both the sameness and the diversity of the created order. She also believes that this highlights a reverse hierarchy in which the most complex creations on the planet are in fact dependent for their continued survival on the lowest forms. It was therefore very bad advice to encourage humans to subdue and dominate creation. Matter, then, is privileged in a way that Christianity has found hard to sustain, for without it nothing else could exist, even mind.[13] Would even Christ exist?

She suggests that we should see the world and God as a continuum and therefore act towards both in the same way. While McFague argues that all that exists is on a continuum she is also able to say that each living thing is both the imago dei and a subject in itself in radical interconnection with all other subjects.[14] Therefore, she encourages Christians to know the world and not flee from it. This knowledge operates in both a big and a small way. The 'big way' takes on the scientific questions and answers and comes to see the world as structured yet open, enduring and novel. The 'small way' assumes the big way and then focuses on the neighbour, be that a tree, a person or a frog.[15] McFague is not arguing for a kind of mystical union with the world, indeed, she sees this as just another way of exploiting it. It is exploitation because we are using the world to back up our feelings rather than seeing it as it is and for itself. Of course, seeing is not as easy as it sounds, since our culture, affected as it is by its Christian heritage, has given us very androcentric, myopic vision. Even if we can see beyond ourselves, we still get stuck at a vision of Christ, that, as we have seen, is not pure or untainted. Nor, significantly, is it less androcentric. McFague is aware of the problems with vision and distinguishes between two types of seeing: seeing with the arrogant eye, and seeing with the loving eye.

---

12. McFague, *The Body of God*, p. 19.

13. McFague, *The Body of God*, p. 42.

14. Sally McFague, *Super Natural Christians: How We Should Love Nature* (London: SCM Press, 1997), pp. 2-3.

15. McFague, *Super Natural Christians*, pp. 20-22.

The arrogant eye sees everything in relation to itself and how all may serve it. To this end it simplifies everything, since, by denying complexity and mystery, it is more able to turn others to its own needs. The loving eye, on the other hand, pays attention to the complexity and diversity in life and sees things quite apart from its own needs and fears.[16] The loving eye is also more earthbound in the sense that it sees things as they really are, without the interference of the distorting self-focused mind. This is not the same as fusing with nature, as it requires much more attention to detail and embracing of diversity. McFague asserts that there are many subjects in the universe and there is no difference between them.

This may seem a totally revolutionary idea, but in fact it is only in recent times that people have viewed nature as an object. During the mediaeval period nature was seen as instructing humans about the ways of God. It was contemplated for the clues it could give to the nature of God and the moral life. It was not seen as mechanistic but as alive with all that was necessary to lead us to a higher understanding. While this is a better attitude to nature than we have today, it was unusual for nature to be valued in itself. In fact while nature may have been lauded in theory it was often demeaned in reality. Despite this the mediaeval period gave people a greater sense of identity with nature as well as a sense of belonging. It is very curious that science fiction is now so popular—is this to fill the gap opened up by our sense of isolation from nature? Do we really need someone out there because we can no longer acknowledge the living 'subjectness' of the earth on which we exist?

McFague is suggesting touch as the radical solution to the ecological crisis. She points out that touch gives us both limits and a sense of interrelationality. It also compels us to face difference and not get lost in 'oceanic feelings of oneness', which can numb us to the real question posed by the world. This relational self/world model is according to McFague a sign of Christian maturity as there is a refusal to retreat from the world or to fuse with it. This model assumes multiple relationships with human and non-human life forms and understands that our experience shapes us. Unlike other feminist theologians McFague is against the notion of fantasy, which she thinks distances us from the reality of people. We merely imagine how they may feel and do not take the time actually to look. She advocates perception based on touch. People are no longer having close encounters with the earth that surround us. This raises all kinds of ethical questions in relation to town planning as well as environmental protection. It was found that during the LA riots in 1992 young

16. McFague, *Super Natural Christians*, p. 34.

people could easily identify automatic weapons by their sound. As McFague notes, 'the interior landscape is influenced by the exterior.'[17] What this seems to suggest is that we need more authentic grounding on the planet if we are to develop as people who can once more feel for it and each other. Ecotheology, then, is beginning to enquire about the urban surroundings of people and not just about the rain forest. The living spaces provided for people will not only have an environmental impact in themselves but will encourage or discourage experiences of the earth. McFague highlights the fact that there are towns and cities that give people good experiences of the earth and emphasizes that she is not looking for a return to the wilderness. We have to create the kingdom around us, but this can be in a garden as much as in the wild.[18]

We can create these 'gardens' by working towards communities that have high levels of literacy and health care and low environmental impact. McFague rightly points out that such communities already exist, Kerala in Southern India being one such community, where, although the income cannot rival that of the USA, the standard of living is high. In other words they are a fine example of lowlevel economy, low environmental impact and a high quality of life. It could be said that they are living lightly on the planet and embodying the kingdom. If McFague spoke specifically christological language she may be suggesting that this form of interrelationality is the essence of Christ. The re-creation of the earth and the people who inhabit it is a historical process that can be seen as redemptive. The Christian focus needs to change from salvation of the individual soul to that of redeeming the earth. This redemption is an unfolding story of people in mutual relation with the whole of the divine/created order.

Strange as it may seem there are pointers to this sensuous connection with the created order in the Genesis story. We are told that knowledge resides in the tree with the luscious fruit, the kind of fruit that one cannot resist touching and savouring. The young male god prohibits the eating of this fruit and dictates that all that people need to know he will tell them. This young male god knows that he has to make this prohibition if he is to remain 'in charge', because once people have known in their bodies, touched, tasted, smelt knowledge, they cannot be easily controlled. The depth of knowledge that the whole body gives empowers people to stand firm in their convictions.

It could be argued that Eve, our foremother, was not disobeying the divine but rather hearing an older divine voice—that of the goddess. In exploring her garden home she was seeking knowledge of it on its own terms and not

---

17. McFague, *Super Natural Christians*, p. 123.
18. McFague, *Super Natural Christians*, p. 160.

according to a 'given', a set of statements handed down from a disembodied Word. She is, then, a model for ecotheology, the one who encourages us to eat of the luscious fruit of the tree of knowledge and savour its goodness. Rather than remove ourselves from the world for the sake of our souls, we should be embracing it as the tangible body of God. This embrace should be one of mutuality not the stranglehold that patriarchy often confuses with affection. We should extend to the world the erotic connection that Heyward advocates between people. In so doing we are engaged in Christic activity. There are two ways of viewing this: either both nature and humans are embracing their own Christic reality through respect, awe and mutuality, or, perhaps more radically, humans are coming to their Christic power through an intimate relationality with God in nature. Both scenarios are far removed from the God/Christ of dualistic metaphysics and so either may provide positive ways ahead for ecotheology.

Both nature and humans are locked in a redemptive dance in which we are out of step. As there is no external Christ and no external guarantee of flourishing, if humans remain so out of step we may be leaving the dance floor sooner, and in a less dignified manner, than anticipated. Indeed, that may be the only way that the cosmos herself can fulfil her divine potential. We had better learn the steps of mutual, erotic embrace fast. We should:

> begin to feel deep respect, even a sense of awe before the life-giving, yet fragile interwovenness of the earth…The rhythmic ebb and flow of the rivers and sea becomes God's dance. The life-giving fecundity of the land with the water is the source of food coming from God's bosom…God energizes the cosmos, and the cosmos in return moves with the creator in a cosmic dance of exquisite balance and beauty.[19]

To include the world in our erotic and embodied process we have to give up the desire for authority and control over. This we can do to the extent that we realise that we are simply part of the process and not the pinnacle of creation. This will enable us to realize that we are part of a bigger whole, and the vulnerability we feel with this realization is just the way it is. We should not seek ways to lessen the tension but simply to live with it. When we realize that nothing is guaranteed we are, paradoxically, in a stronger position than when living in theological Disney world where the good guys get their reward in the end. To abandon dualistic thinking places the emphasis more squarely on the here and now and frees us to seek empowerment-in-relation with all that is around us. Instead of looking for the divine beyond what we see we have to

---

19. Chung Hyun Kyung in David Hallman, *Ecotheology: Voices from South and North* (Maryknoll, NY: Orbis Books, 1994), p. 177.

pay more attention to what we see in order to engage bodily with the divine in its diversity around and within us. Christians have to come to terms with the stark reality that redemption does not lie beyond this world and this body but within both. Ecotheology is a theology of redemption and not just an ethical issue tagged on at the end of Christian systematic theology. By placing the tree from Eden rather that that from Calvary at the centre of a theology of redemption, it is hoped that people will embrace the reality of the here and now. Further it will show that the garden has yet to be understood and nurtured rather than a harvest already planted has just to be cut and gathered. There is a process unfolding, and the tree that was once the symbol of fallenness is best reimaged as that of our ecological future, if that unfolding is to preserve the planet and its inhabitants. The ecological Christ is very much a Christ of liberation and not a mystical wish fulfiller. We are not given the luxury of contemplating the majesty of God in a world drowning under pollution and environmental carnage; instead, we are called to action.

Walking the Road With Jesus

Ivone Gebara, like others, is compelled to search for answers to the ecological crisis that show the connections between pollution, hunger and unemployment and the patriarchal image of God.[20] This is a feminist project because women do the cleaning up while men spend their time getting things dirty, and it is a liberation project because the poor do not make the most waste but often have to live amid it, as dumps of all kinds are placed on their doorstep. Gebara is not romanticizing either the poor or women but is just describing what she sees in her country, Brazil. What she does argue is that women and nature as well as the poor are included in the process of knowledge-making, and that it is not left to educated and wealthy elites to decide what is the way ahead. We have to think differently and this has to originate from the margins. If we begin from the earth as a margin, we find that we even think differently about war. She argues that ecological cost is great in war yet it is never considered; nature is used as both a weapon and a victim. Although we count the dead, we rarely if ever, count the ecological cost. Our patriarchal way of knowing denies what we see in favour of preconceived ideals into which what we observe has to fit. This is as much the case with theological knowing as with ways of counting the cost of war. Gebara argues that an ecofeminist way of knowing is not interested in such denial and manipulation, rather, it

---

20. Ivone Gebara, *Longing for Running Water: Ecofeminism and Liberation* (Philadelphia: Fortress Press, 1999), p. 1.

acknowledges that all objects are contained in the subject and the subject is both subject and object.[21] There is interdependence in knowing that male logic denies. We cannot then divide humans and the earth as though they were separate thought categories but should rather approach both as fundamental and integral to ecological questions and answers. Ecojustice, then, is grounded in an affirmation of our bodies as part of the sacred body of the earth and our relatedness is also earthy and does not rely on some transcendent reality.

Gebara's general framework poses interesting questions for Christology and she is not slow to take up the challenge. She declares that the place that Jesus occupies in the Christian community should no longer be understood as an absolute dogmatic reference point but rather he should be seen in a more participatory way, more dialogical and open.[22] (We begin to understand why Sr Ivone has not always found favour with the Vatican!) Gebara compares Jesus to the food that our grandmothers made, dishes that will always be special to us and that we can go back to in our memories when we try something similar, but we can never reproduce their recipes. We have to discard that kind of dogma, since it is dogma that took a conversation by a well, a shared meal and a caress and turned them into systematic reason. Dogma 'made a prison out of an invitation to freedom'.[23] Gebara wants to move away from patriarchal readings of Scripture that encourage dependence, that is, we are supposed to think that Jesus dispenses all the gifts. She thinks this model is disempowering for Latin America and she reminds us that women brought the food that was multiplied and made the bread that was blessed; this is not a one-way street in terms of salvific action.

Gebara highlights how we see something of the nature of Jesus' understanding of life through his insistence that people believe in themselves. His role in this was to help restore them to health and dignity at times through providing the basic essentials of life, food and drink. He demonstrates a practical wisdom that shows that certain needs have to be met in the moment and not put off for some future eschaton. Gebara argues that the ecological crisis demands just such practical wisdom. The earth has been enslaved by economic exploitation and so it has to become the subject and object of salvation. The principles we see at work in Jesus and his relationship with people need to be extended to the earth not in order that he becomes its redeemer but that we may act with it in divine solidarity. Gebara agrees with McFague that in order to affirm the incarnation one does not have to give Jesus a unique

---

21. Gebara, *Longing for Running Water*, p. 53.
22. Gebara, *Longing for Running Water*, p. 178.
23. Gebara, *Longing for Running Water*, p. 178.

character, rather, he too is our sacred body yet the incarnation spreads far beyond him and us.[24] Jesus may, however, be a metaphor for the divine presence in all things.

For Gebara Jesus is a saviour in so far as he stands for those values that will enable us to make changes for goodness and justice. He represents a process of salvation that can be assumed by men and women whose 'hearts are tilled with mercy and solidarity.'[25] Jesus/Christ is, for Gebara, a symbol and as such moves beyond the man from Nazareth and becomes a possession of the community of followers, a path to meaning. The man of Nazareth was constrained by cultural expectations and understandings but the symbol can move far beyond historical moments and is a partner in a dialogue in which we include ourselves and by definition our own time and space. Gebara is not arguing in the classical sense about the Jesus of history and the Christ of faith, she is instead finding practical Christology for a world in ecological crisis. She considers that a Christ who provides enough symbolism for life giving and flourishing of dignity gives the collective authority to speak in different ways about our experiences of Jesus. The real world does not act as though it were a metaphysical construct; it is rather messy and imperfect, full of contradictions, and above all else in need of human support. Jesus stands as a symbol of orthopraxis in such a world and as such is bound to be more flexible than the Christ of dogma. Dogma is failing to respond to the demands of our historical moment, and it remains to be seen if the symbolic, embedded Christ can.

Gebara, of course, moves far away from the sacrificed and suffering Christ, since this is a symbol that does not prove useful for our ecological needs. I have to agree that it is no longer useful to pin our ecological hopes on the tree on Calvary and I have long advocated a return to the tree in Eden as the one that provides us with a sound ecological model. The engaged and sensuous relation that we see between Eve and her surroundings stands in stark contrast to the remote model of heroic suffering portrayed by Christian doctrine. The future would seem to depend on the sacrifice of hierarchies and a more embodied engagement with the world and each other, and I remain unconvinced that Calvary offers such a model.

Green Christic Eschatons

Feminist theologians have placed Christ at the centre of ecotheology both as redeemer and redeemed, seeing nature as part of the covenanted cosmos.

---

24. Gebara, *Longing for Running Water*, p. 184.
25. Gebara, *Longing for Running Water*, p. 186.

Ruether[26] and Halkes[27] both envisage a world in which people and nature live side by side in harmony. All is flourishing and the fullness of life is available to all, human and animal alike. This picture is not thought to be one that is beyond the capabilities of humankind. Since humans have wrought destruction they can, through a metanoia, also usher in another reality, one with peace at its heart. Elisabeth Green[28] wonders why, despite their optimism and utopian dreams, ecofeminists stop short of declaring that death too can be overcome. Most simply accept it as part of being alive and invest it with no great religious significance, that is to say, it is not the time when one meets one's maker. Green is puzzled because Christian eschatology has not been kind to women or nature. Both have been said to disappear in the hereafter, women becoming men and angels and nature being replaced by disembodied salvation. Even so-called evolutionary theologians have suggested that matter becomes spiritualized and therefore ceases to exist. Feminist theologians, who are always working to overcome dualistic thinking, should not give in to the inherent dualism in eschatological thought but should find alternatives.

Green suggests that Sophia is a good starting point, since she was in the beginning, makes all things new as well as sustaining the earth. She also draws our attention to the way in which we are told the earth reacted at the death of Christ Sophia on the cross: the earth was plunged into darkness but this signalled the birth pains of a new creation. This new creation included the whole of creation, not just the faithful. Green links this new creation with the resurrection, which she reminds us was physical, and concludes that bodies matter. If we just see these events as symbolic, Green believes that we lose a very important component of Christianity, and that is embodiment. We simply disappear into a rather ethereal evolutionary process and are gone. Green asserts that there is more to redemptive theology than that. She believes that affirming the resurrection of the body actually helps to counter some of the more body-denying aspects of Christian theology as well as allowing for the diversity of humankind and nature to continue to shine in all its glory. Further, in a very concrete way, it allows for the continuation of relationality, which includes the earth. Green believes that her argument is cosmic,

26. Rosemary Ruether, *Gaia and God: An Ecofeminist Theology of Earth Healing* (San Francisco: Harper & Row, 1992).

27. Catharina Halkes, *New Creation: Christian Feminism and the Renewal of the Earth* (London: SCM Press, 1991).

28. Elisabeth Green, 'The Travail of Creation and the Daughters of God: Ecofeminism and Eschatology', in *Feminist Theology* 14 (Sheffield: Sheffield Academic Press, 1994), pp. 44-56.

corporeal and collective, in short, it is a feminist argument and one that overcomes some of the weaknesses in current feminist theology.

While I appreciate what she is attempting to do, I think that she does not give full credit to those, such as Ruether, who are truly dissolving dualism by seeing little difference between this life and the life of cosmic compost. Green is not alone in thinking that abandoning ideas about resurrection is conceding too much. Elisabeth Stuart suggests that eschatons allow us to sustain 'big visions', that is, we have a place to stand beyond the mire of present reality. This, however, is a rather different idea and one that does not overtly include creation. Green has made a very valid point but I am not sure that she has adequately answered it. In what way should humans overcome death in order that dualism and hierarchy should not be reintroduced? Nature does indeed regenerate itself but parts of it do become extinct or simply continue to exist through reproduction. Where do humans fit? There is a danger that if we reintroduce resurrection we once again place humans outside the created order in a quite unwarranted place of privilege.

Our Own Vineyards; Our Own Vines: Feminist Futures

Once women start theological reflection from their own embodied experience and from the earth the face of theology changes. Nothing can be left untouched by such rooted theology. The risk of incarnation is a huge one and to date Christianity has avoided that risk and has instead found comfort and security in a dualistic world and an almighty God. The result has been reassuring for individual Christians and devastating for the planet and the non-human world. Ecofeminism is keen not to over-romanticize the relation-ship between women and nature but sees the beginnings of a conversion to the earth lying in an honouring and reinstating of women as the image of God. The healing of women from the patriarchal wounds inflicted over centuries and the healing of the scars on the earth and in the sky are not seen as separate issues. Women and the cosmos are claiming their divine/Christic nature in order to find healing and to demand justice. Christ can no longer be squeezed into doctrinal formulas and controlled by the power of clergy, she is throbbing in the whole of creation, and women, the great sustainers of life, are alive with the same Christic energy that pounds through their mothers' veins.

Chapter Five

Suffering Christ

It may not surprise readers that this chapter is shorter than the rest. After all the image of a Christ who suffers has, in large part, been used against women. It is this Christ who was writ large in the minds of spiritual directors who advised women to mutilate their bodies for Jesus who was said to take pleasure in it.[1] Combined with a notion of self-sacrificial love suffering has reduced, and at times claimed, the lives of many Christian women over the centuries. These women have devoted themselves to churches that have historically treated them as barely human, yet they have continued to provide social services that have cost them dear. Sadly this is not a story left in the past, a piece of mediaeval history, mourned and best forgotten. Domestic violence is reaching epidemic levels—more women suffer annually at the hands of 'loved ones' than from cancer, heart disease and car accidents combined—yet the churches remain silent. More grotesquely they will not engage with the theology that allows such violence in Christian homes or that makes space for priests and Christian counsellors to advise women to 'go home and place your suffering alongside Jesus'. Vicarious suffering has been seen as meritorious within Christianity and it is this combined with notions of male superiority that places women and children at risk within Christian homes.[2] In addition there is virtual silence regarding women's low pay, protection of prostitutes, rights of workers in sweat shops and many other ills that afflict women and cause then undue suffering. There are no 'goods of suffering' but the churches are slow to accept this. However, as Christian theologians feminists cannot simply abandon ideas that have been central to Christian understanding without at least attempting to subvert them!

1.   See Karen Armstrong, *The Gospel According to Woman* (London: Pan, 1986), for more on these pornographic assaults on the bodies of women in the name of holiness.

2.   Isherwood, 'Marriage Haven or Hell'.

Feminist christological hermeneutics are orientated to liberation praxis and therefore hold biblical stories responsible for shaping public reality. Therefore, exploration of biblical texts does not begin with the text itself but with a critical articulation and analysis of the experiences of women. How have the texts affected reality and how does that impact on the lives of women? Fiorenza is aware that none cause more problems than those that have led to a theology of the cross. In the last century Elisabeth Cady Stanton pointed out that Eve, the founding mother of sin, and a male saviour were intertwined problems for women. Mary Daly, as we have seen, took up the point by showing that Eve, the cross and the sacrificial nature of Jesus encouraged women to be scapegoated and to remain passive about that scapegoating. Elisabeth Moltmann-Wendel and Mary Grey have tried to re-image atonement and redemption in such a way that it will speak to feminists positively. Wendel sees the cross as a paradoxical symbol of life while Grey wishes to reinvent atonement as at-one-ment and suggest relational mutuality.

While Heyward and Soelle[3] no longer see the cross as anything other than a political tool, the means by which many died in order to try and subdue a people, it has no redemptive, atoning function. Further, as Brock points out, Christologies that are about submission 'sanction child abuse on a cosmic scale'. By ritualizing the suffering of Jesus, kyriarchal power protects itself from those who may otherwise object to their own suffering. By making his death non-political, the status quo can preserve itself. However, if we see his death as political and image the resurrection as the presence of Jesus 'going before you to Galilee' [a place of political dissent], then the cross does not support kyriarchal power but actually undermines it and makes it look to texts for its own validation. While western women may wish to downplay or reinvent the suffering of Jesus this may not be the whole story.

The Christ of Han-Pu-Ri

Asian women theologians are committed to creating theology from their own context, using indigenous folk literature, traditions and lived experience. They are open to the possibilities of exploring theology through poems, dance and rituals, and they realize that in so doing they will be challenging basic elements of western Christian theology. The embodied memory that most carry of this new and exciting approach is from the Assembly of the World Council of Churches held in Canberra in 1991. The Korean theologian Chung Hyun Kyung gave a plenary paper accompanied by drums, dance and ritual, some of

3.   D. Soelle, *Theology for Sceptics: Reflections on God* (Philadelphia: Fortress Press, 1995).

which was modelled on the Han-pu-ri ceremonies from her country. Within this embodied illustration she spoke of the need to create a dramatic paradigm shift in doing theology, one that allowed her pain as an Asian woman to be addressed. Asian women's theology is narrative in that it emerges from the ongoing story and is not rooted in the already told and fossilized universalist tale.

Telling their story has deep roots in Korean culture, particularly in Han-pu-ri, which comes from a shamanistic background. Han is a 'root experience' of the Korean people because it signifies their oppression and the 'lump' in their spirit that has ensued. They feel resentment because of the injustices they have suffered and have a feeling of helplessness and total abandonment. There is a deep desire for revenge in the sense of putting things right.[4] Women have experienced their own unique kind of han, moving as they have from more or less equal status in ancient Korea to a place of silence and second-class citizenship in modern times. Women in Korea suffer sexual violence as well as a wide range of abuses both within and outside the home. Many of the women who are sexually abused decide to kill themselves because of the culture of shame that surrounds them. Christianity has not in any significant way altered the lot of Korean women, which is unsurprising, existing as it does in a culture that is deeply affected by other traditions. This is not to suggest that Christianity would, left to itself, be the liberator of women as we have seen this is not always the case. It is not surprising that many Korean Christian women are looking towards their own traditions as well as Christianity to provide liberating alternatives.

Han-pu-ri is one place they look. It is a ritual carried out by shamans who are usually women and its purpose is to give voice to ghosts or people who have no other way of being heard. Once they have been heard the source of their oppression has to be named and action has to be decided that will overcome the oppressive situation. It is hardly surprising to learn that a large number of the shamans and participants are women, since this is one of the few ways in which oppressed women can get together away from the gaze of men and tell their stories. They speak to a listening audience who will then help them find ways to improve their situation. In allowing women a voice the ceremonies also provide a creative space in which women can find ways to resist and overcome their suffering.

Chung Hyun Kyung argues that women's han has to be the starting point

---

4.   See Chung Hyun Kyung, 'Han-pu-ri: Doing Theology from a Korean Woman's Perspective', in Virginia Fabella and Sun Ai Lee Park (eds.), *We Dare to Dream* (Hong Kong: AWCCT, 1989), pp. 60-72.

for theology in Korea. In this way she is not unlike other feminist theologians who understand the lived experience of women to be the place that all theological reflection has to start. Of course, the experience of women in Korea is unique to them and so the outcome of their reflection will be distinct. They have not simply experienced oppression but also resistance, that is, they have also acted as liberators. Both oppression and resistance require a process of critical reflection in order to untangle the webs of abuse that impinge on the lives of women. Therefore, reflection coupled with critical engagement with tradition act as two more links in the creation of women's theology. (Many Asian women do not use the term feminist in relation to themselves and their theology, as they see this as just one more western construct that they do not wish to have imposed upon them.) Korean women also use texts in a radical way, going behind the stories and beyond them to meet the community that exists in the written word. From their experience they know that what may be a liberating word for men may not act in the same way for women. Therefore, it is the women in the text that they look for and even their absence is viewed as significant. Korean women judge as good theology anything that liberates them from han and empowers them.[5] These same standards are applied to Christology, a good Christ addresses han and liberates.

Perhaps the most powerful image of Jesus for Korean women is as shaman. Shamanism always played a positive role in the lives of women as it presented an alternative to the patriarchal realities of Confucianism and other religions. The shaman functioned as an intermediary between the spirit world of the ancestors and individuals or families. They were able to exorcise demons and carry out rituals believed to change the families luck. For this reason the shaman held a high position in society, and many shamans were women. Korean women are able to understand Jesus as a shaman because of his exorcisms and healings, which is very familiar territory for them, since as shamans they are themselves exorcists and healers. They are therefore able to identify with Jesus through their own actions. Of course, healing and exorcism both suggest that suffering is to be overcome and not embraced as salvific. The shaman engages with the sick and the psychologically disturbed to restore health and balance. Christ the shaman is, then, closely related to Jesus of Nazareth: she embraces those who are suffering and she heals them. Jesus then is identified as a big sister, just as the shaman is, and not as Lord of all and the only Son of God.[6]

This female identification of Jesus is carried through the connections made

5.   Chung, 'Han-pu-ri', p. 65.
6.   Chung, 'Han-pu-ri', p. 66.

between him and Kuan Yin. Kuan Yin is the compassionate goddess of the commonfolk who symbolizes relatedness, community and suffering. She is a celestial bodhisattva who hears the cries of the world.[7] She is also a personification of wisdom and appears to people who are in need. Her suffering is connected with her wisdom and is seen as redemptive but in a radically different way from that of Jesus. Kuan Yin is a wise sufferer, that is, she may walk a painful path because she sees the radical possibilities for change by so doing. This is a powerful message for women who often suffer for no good reason and have not believed that transformation should be the goal of their suffering. If Korean women get a better perspective on their own suffering through the combination of their own culture with that of Christianity, they become able to see their own position as one of transformative, redemptive suffering. The Korean imaging of Christ from below means that a hero or a mighty ruler would be an inappropriate understanding of the one who would be called saviour in the Korean context. Christ does not arrive triumphant in the lives of the oppressed but rather,

> emerges from the broken-body experience of workers when they affirm life and dare to love other human beings in spite of their brokenness. Workers become Christ to each other when they touch each other's wounds and heal each other through sharing food, work and hope.[8]

The sharing of these resources, particularly food, is another way in which the embodied Christ is understood. He is the grain since it is the grain that gives them life. For starving people the greatest love and redemption bestowed by God is the next grain of rice. It hardly needs pointing out that the traditional host, the so-called body of Christ, lacking in substance as it does and dispensed as it is from on high by the one with the power, is not a useful or powerful image in Korean circumstances. They require something that comes up from the ground and is shared by those who have no power except for a communal will to live.

However, many Korean women do start with Jesus as their co-sufferer. Imaged as the Suffering Servant they believe that he is able to know their true feelings and empathize with them. This is an image that seems to speak to most women theologians in Korea wherever they sit on the theological spectrum. This model shouts loudly that domination is never right, and it is this message that the women need to hear. They are also able to find meaning in

7.   Naomi F. Southard, 'Recovery and Rediscovered Images: Spiritual Resources for Asian American Women', in Ursula King (ed.), *Feminist Theology from the Third World* (London: SPCK, 1994), pp. 378-91 (383).

8.   Chung, *Struggle to be the Sun Again* (London: SCM Press, 1990), p. 7.

their own suffering not in the traditional way of supposing it will bring them rewards in heaven but by viewing it as redemptive for others just as Jesus' suffering was said to be. There are always dangers involved in seeing suffering as positive because one runs the risk of sacrificing oneself into oblivion. Chung Hyun Kyung is aware of the particular dangers for Korean women, seeing that they have had a very mixed message about suffering both from their own culture and from the colonizers. She fears that some may find it easier to accept the Suffering Servant role in the traditional sense snce this is all they have ever known. They are encouraged to love Jesus and to suffer while he seems largely absent from their lives. Chung wonders if this is the only model they know, as it is reminiscent of their fathers, husbands and lovers.[9] Those who reject this model also find the courage to reject other relationships of the same kind. Their courage comes from the respect that they feel Jesus affords them and the sense of self-worth and dignity that this brings to their lives. Strangely, this respect can be argued to come from the image of Jesus as suffering servant: he went through what they go through and came out with dignity. The women believe that they can do the same. It is this dignity that provides hope for the future. They may be oppressed but they are still engaged in redemptive praxis for themselves and others by envisioning dignity and freedom.

Jesus the Corn Mother

First Nations theologians, like other colonized people, have much to ponder in relation to the Christ of conquest. It was only in the 1970s that the last residential schools for First Nations children was closed in Canada. These mainly religious foundations took children away from their homes as early as four years old and declared that they would 'Christianize and civilize' them. In short they would remove their culture, dignity and sense of belonging.[10] As so often happens sexual and physical abuse was rampant in these institutions. In addition, the education that was supposed to make a difference in their lives was at a lower level than promised and so delivered even the brightest children into the world as low-paid workers. These acts of cultural genocide sit on top of decades of actual genocide in which the indigenous peoples of the Americas

---

9.   Chung, *Struggle*, p. 54

10.   Gladys Taylor Cooke, an elder of the Dakota tribe, suffered horribly in such an institution. She tells with amazement how her hair was cut and her rituals banned along with her language, while she was put in a kilt and taught Scottish dancing. This was put on as entertainment for admiring whites.

were hounded, killed, infected with killer diseases[11] and squeezed into small areas of land that could not sustain them. It is not surprising that many First Nations theologians have declared Christ to be a dangerous concept for indigenous people.

However, others choose to engage and reclaim the power of the concept for themselves. Within indigenous cultures there are many ceremonies connected with vicarious suffering, the Sun Dance, the Rite of Vigil or Vision Quest and the Purification Ceremony or Sweat Lodge. Almost every tribe in North America has a variety of ceremonies that involve the individual in vicarious suffering for the whole people. The first missionaries viewed these rituals as demonic and declared that they fell short of the supreme example of Christ. In alienating First Nations people from their rituals the missionaries not only exerted colonial domination but also insisted on a profoundly different view of God and the world.

While Christianity has inherent in Jesus' suffering the notion of an angry God, First Nations found such a concept to be too anthropomorphic. For them vicarious suffering is a very human activity that helps reset the balance necessary for harmonious life on the planet. They understand the Sacred Energy to be inherent in all things and to be a force for good. However, individuals do not always work with this energy and so various rituals were devised as a way of realigning oneself with the planet and one's people. The ceremonies celebrate the willingness of individuals to do their part in the work of the planet; they do not glorify suffering but rather dance the reintegration. Therefore, in as much as individuals are suffering for others, they are also suffering for themselves. They do not directly save others through this suffering and by divine grace, but grace and salvation can be seen at work in this model. By engaging in activities that speak of reinstating balance people are once more committing themselves to the flourishing of people and planet. This is not grounded in notions of atonement at a metaphysical level but is a fully grounded and active engagement with real need. The colonial 'Mr Fix-It' is replaced by a spiritually/politically active people working for and with the Sacred Energy.

What we come to realize here is that many emerging Christologies do not have as their guiding force an innate desire to conform to a Euro-centric logic. Indeed, First Nations history warns against such a thing. What we see instead are spiritual traditions which have their own uniqueness engaging with an alien and alienating tradition with respect in order to find new understandings.

---

11. Not only did illness that was harmless to whites kill large numbers, but infected blankets were sent to Indian women and children in deliberate acts of germ warfare.

Even so-called liberal ideas about the Cosmic Christ cannot hold this emerging explosion to self-determination and spiritual affirmation on the part of those so cruelly treated by the conveyers of the colonial Christ.

The gender, not only the colonial power, of Christ is problematic for First Nations people. The Sacred Energy is understood as both male and female; which means that 'because of our experience of ultimate reality as a bi-gender duality, any equivalent for the Euro-Christian Christ would include examples that are explicitly female'.[12] One such image would be the Corn Mother, which can be conceived of as christological. The Corn Mother is the first mother who willingly gives of herself for her children She provides food by shaking the corn from her own body and allowing them to eat it. In some stories her children kill her, although she is willing for this to happen. The first mother is buried and becomes the source of enduring fecundity of the earth and vegetable foods; she nourishes her children for all eternity with her body.

There are obvious sacramental parallels with Christianity, but the big difference is that, in gratefully eating from the mother's body First Nations people are drawn closer to the earth not propelled further from it. Corn and all other foods are our relations and draw us into communion with animals who, like us, gain their strength from eating the body of their mother. In addition eating joins us to those who have died, our ancestors, since they have returned to the earth and become part of what nourishes us today.

Willing self-sacrifice of Corn Mother is not only enacted symbolically but also acts as an ethical imperative for those in the community who continue to fight for indigenous land rights, education and recognition within the churches. She alone did not die for all, but her example makes demands of people, demands for communal life, even if there is personal cost. Some of the stories associated with Corn Mother tell of her being killed by young men. This is used to demonstrate the necessity for controlling male aggression and assertiveness in the community.

We see emerging a very different model despite the fact that willing sacrifice is at the heart of this indigenous christological tale. The story and the sacramental imaging are strikingly similar yet the world vision is light years apart. By continuing to engage with their own traditions in the wake of crushing colonialization indigenous people are attempting to find healing for themselves and the colonizers who are not left entirely unbrutalized by their

12. George Tinker, 'Jesus, Corn Mother and Conquest', in Jace Weaver (ed.), *Native American Religious Identity* (Maryknoll, NY: Orbis Books, 1998).

own brutish behaviour and mind sets. By broadening the debate, new hori-
zons of mutual understanding open up as possibilities and Christic moments.

And None but Jesus Heard Me

Womanist theology has its roots in the suffering of black people in America.
Their history, so embedded in the inhumanity of slavery, screams with pain,
indignity, death and the stifling suffering of powerlessness. The words of
Sojourner Truth that head this section make the situation plain. When she was
whipped, when her children were sold into slavery and ripped from her, when
she was overworked and underfed and when she cried out in her pain none
but Jesus heard her. We can then imagine that if there were anything good to
be said about suffering we would hear it from womanists. However, as we
have already seen, womanist theology engages with God and the world in a
very positive way. It does not romanticize or glamorize the suffering of the
Sojourner's of this world, it names the activities that cause the suffering as evil.
Systems that do not promote and protect the dignity of the individual are
called to repent of their innate sinfulness through turning to justice-making.

The emphasis on wholeness and life-affirming action in womanist theology
presents problems for womanist theologians when they consider traditional
models of atonement. The notion that Jesus died for us is not a healthy
paradigm in a community in which coercion and suffering for the benefits of
others has been a harsh and lived reality. Douglas is not alone in declaring that
a new understanding of this central doctrine has to be sought.[13] She is also
fully aware that many within the black community actually find it strangely
comforting to be able to identify with the suffering of Christ and to feel that
he saw, and sees, theirs. However, Douglas reminds us that black people in
slavery who declared that Jesus was their liberator knew nothing of Nicene
creeds. Their declaration was firmly based in the reality of the here and now
and not in metaphysical theology. What they believed Jesus could do for them
in the dire reality of everyday life was the crucial thing. This Christ, then, was
not one to be set aside for worship but was in the nitty-gritty of life and the
transformative power of following his actions was emphasized. This has meant
that womanists have developed an understanding of Christ that can never
move far from the realities of the lives of ordinary black women.[14] While many
womanists make a connection between Jesus' suffering and that of women
they are also keen not to let his suffering obscure theirs. Alice Walker places a

13. See also the work of Delores Williams and Jacquelyn Grant.
14. Kelly Brown Douglas, *The Black Christ* (Maryknoll, NY: Orbis Books, 1994), p. 114.

plea in the mouth of one of her characters, Tashi, that the suffering of women should be the focus of sermons rather than the long ago suffering of Jesus. Tashi asks, 'Was woman herself not the tree of life? And was she not crucified? Not in some age no one remembers, but right now, daily, in many lands'.[15]

Of course this requires a major shift in the Christian understanding of suffering. Delores Williams[16] challenges the notions of surrogacy and structural domination innate in traditional interpretations. Jesus is released to glory by his suffering while black women are imprisoned in theirs yet encouraged to believe that suffering is somehow sacred. In identifying women with the tree of life crucified, womanists are careful not to glorify this identification. Rather they look for the end of suffering and the full flourishing of their lives in this world. Christ is then the suffering healer and the one who releases others into abundant life.

There is no doubt that the suffering Christ was an empowerer for many black women, just as he is for some in Korea today. The fact that such an image is viewed with caution by many contemporary womanists is a good example of how context is everything. Womanist who have more control over their lives than even their grandmothers did are not keen to place their trust in the suffering Messiah since this figure could neutralize their energy for change. As they feel they have more power to change the inequalities still perpetrated on their people they look less to the passive sufferer and more towards the Christ of black pride and justice.

Christ the Midwife

Like other countries and peoples on the receiving end of colonialism and the imperial Christ, Africans are very cautious about embracing a suffering Christ. It was this Christ who encouraged them to know their place when sold into slavery and has since encouraged them to grin and bear it while their country has been ravaged by colonial and multinational greed. It is this Christ they encounter in the lives of the millions of AIDS sufferers on the continent, and it is this Christ who has limited power to save.

An important aspect of Christ in Africa is his ability to heal the cosmos as well as ease the suffering of individuals. Many who feel empowered by a suffering Christ are in fact healers and exorcists who understand that the suffering Christ calls for healing because liberation involves physical and

15. Alice Walker, *Possessing the Secret of Joy* (New York: Harcourt Brace Jovanovich, 1993), p. 274.

16. Williams, *Sisters in the Wilderness*, p. 169.

psychological health. While Christ in this context will understand suffering, he will also conspire against it, since he is a holistic Christ and not a man of sorrows. Indeed, only such holism will suffice on a continent that has been so dismembered by the imposition of the imperial Christ.

On a continent where physical suffering seems endemic, a suffering Christ is still a very attractive prospect for some because he could champion their cause. However, the African mind set understands suffering as birth pangs, which means it has to lead to new beginnings. In this sense Christ's suffering is a midwife to the new.[17]

This Christ who births the new also questions world structures that impoverish Africa and lie at the heart of much of its suffering. In short, this Christ draws theologians into socio-political-economic analysis and requires them to speak against the manmade forces that impose suffering on an already bleeding continent. Many of those who speak out will themselves have to endure some suffering due to their outspokenness. However, it is not their actions and suffering that are viewed as salvific but rather their vision of a new social order. For the women of Africa there is no distinction between salvation and liberation. The cross can never be the end point and they look always for the resurrection in the everyday lives of people and in the soil of Africa. The suffering Christ is part of the process but by no means the end point of a salvific journey.

The Disabled Christ

Can we imagine that the perfect God of dualistic metaphysics and the equally untainted Son could be disabled? [18] Why was Jesus not a quadriplegic, and why did God not stammer when uttering the words of creation? Despite some biblical evidence that may suggest otherwise, God/Christ cannot be viewed as mentally disabled either. This may seem rather flippant but it is not without theological significance. Had the Christian God been understood to be disabled the history of disabled people within Christianity would have been rather different. Because Christians have viewed God as perfect in every way, they have to their eternal shame, viewed disability as imperfect and at times demonic. It is too easy to say they just did not understand in times gone by, but what excuse is there today for fundamentalists dragging people out of

---

17. For more on this see Mercy Amba Oduyoye, *Introducing African Women's Theology* (Sheffield: Sheffield Academic Press, 2001).

18. Nancy Eiesland, *The Disabled God: Toward a Liberatory Theology of Disability* (Nashville: Abingdon Press, 1994), p. 93.

wheelchairs while yelling for any number of named demons to leave them. This disturbing scene was shown on television as part of a series that followed fundamentalist preachers touring Britain; the model of disability as a sign of sin was well in place among those who gathered by the thousand to express their devotion to Christ. Women with disabilities have carried an extra burden, since they are viewed as doubly transgressive. Many of those burnt as witches had no greater deformity than a third nipple, the so-called 'devil's teat'. The conflation of sin and disability is a devastating error that Christianity would do well to repent. Emerging images of a disabled Christ may be the first positive aspect of this repentance. Empowering symbols are important to all marginalized groups and there is a certain satisfaction in subverting a symbol that has been part of historic oppression.

Nancy Eiesland is one of the first theologians to attempt to develop a theology of disability, and once again this is ahead of the churches which have not really begun to grasp the issues involved in disabled civil rights. There is still, to their shame, reluctance in some churches to ordain people with disabilities. This is of course a direct result of viewing God as perfect and therefore insisting that his representatives also mirror that perfection.

Disabled theology, like feminist theology before it, starts with the body and uses it as a positive place to begin theological reflection. Those who have been imaged as the modern-day 'virtuous sufferers' have been swamped by Christian charity, which, however well meant, has acted in a disabling way. It springs from an able-bodied mind set that assumes that those who are differently abled have to be 'done unto'. This kind of paternalism gives little respect to the abilities and ambitions of the disabled, rather it attempts to make compliant children out of them so that we may all the more find some reason for their suffering. It becomes the suffering of the sweet innocent and is easily aligned with that of Jesus. By refusing to be limited by these stereotypes and engaging with the symbol of Christ the Suffering Servant disabled theologians pose challenges for theology and for the 'rituals of degradation' carried out by the 'caring'. These include avoidance of eye contact, speaking for or about a disabled person when in their company and a strange fascination with the bodies of the disabled. All these modes of engagement are fuelled by basic Christian concepts, such as virtuous suffering or segregational charity, and not least the connection of sin and suffering. All these approaches will coopt people with disabilities into their own oppression, that is, they help foster low self-esteem and dependency.

While gay theologians encourage 'acting up', Eiesland urges 'acting out', which she describes as a theological method that joins political action with resymbolization. It is the enactment of holding bodies together in societies filled with overt discrimination. The political action involves equal rights and access campaigning as well as face-to-face encounters with those who operate from the level of unthinking stereotypes. In short, acting out is the revolutionary work of resistance to acquiescence. Of course, this means coming to terms with bodies and their sometimes disagreeable aspects. This is not all celebration and can demand a huge price in terms of realistic engagement. Eiesland talks about 'survive-able' bodies, which are those that refuse to be self-flagellating because they do not fit the standard norm but instead learn to live with the pain and pleasure of being who they are. She rightly points out that, in a society that wants us to engage with the obsessive quest for perfect bodies, this act of self-worth and self-love is an act of resistance and liberation.

Fundamental to this process is solidarity with others who are disabled and a refusal to play the game of the 'good' and the 'bad' disabled. This sense of solidarity extends globally and poses questions about disability as a result of malnutrition or torture. It is thought that there are about 600 million people who are disabled worldwide, and malnutrition is the cause of at least 20 per cent of it. A theology of disability therefore calls for relief from the causes of the pain. In addition there is a pacifist agenda, that wishes to eliminate disability caused by the body-ripping realities of war.

It is the disabled Christ who sits at the centre of this theology and who acts as the moral imperative for these things to be striven for. God became flesh, and flesh, as we know, comes in all shapes, sizes and with a wide range of ability and disability. For Eiesland it is the resurrected Christ who is a theological starting point, since 'in the resurrected Jesus Christ, they saw not the suffering servant for whom the last word was tragedy and sin, but the disabled God who embodied both impaired hands and feet and pierced side and the imago Dei.'[19] The disabled God is not the One from heaven but is a real person with all the variety that this implies. In revealing a physically impaired resurrected body, all kinds of taboos are broken. The body that is impaired is not untouchable or unlovable but is 'a new model of wholeness and a symbol of solidarity.'

Eiesland highlights how the disabled Christ also goes some way to alleviating the feminist concern over the maleness of Christ. The disabled Christ is not a suffering servant or an imperial Lord but rather is weak and an outcast. In addition the emphasis in this model is on physicality and not maleness. This Christ is not a 'fixer' either but is rather a survivor, which may be an

19. Eiesland, *The Disabled God*, p. 99.

encouraging image for some women. While I can appreciate Eiesland's position I am not convinced that it does in fact make the image of Christ more palatable for women. It certainly does challenge the more Rambo images of Christ that we have been used to, but I feel it is too optimistic to think that we can image physicality without imaging gender. There is no doubt that Christ as survivor is a powerful one but it could also encourage resignation to abuse in the knowledge that women and Christ survive. This is not to say that it has no place, it is an image that works well in our broken world, although it may not be an image that underpins our utopian vision.

The disabled Christ highlights the necessity for mutuality and interdependence, the latter being a condition of the lives of many disabled people. We are offered a Christ who needs care and mutuality for survival. We have a similar notion in the Christology of Carter Heyward, when she suggests that the divine can die due to lack of interrelationality. While challenging the oppressive model of an all-powerful God, it also questions individualism and human hierarchy. Our society perpetuates the myth that the truly capable person needs no one and moves beyond interdependence, but the disabled model challenges this and draws us back to humanity. Above all else the disabled Christ is a symbol 'of rightly ordered interpersonal and structural relations.'

Elisabeth Stuart picks up on Eiesland's claim that 'Jesus Christ the disabled God disorders the social-symbolic orders of what it means to be incarnate.'[20] Stuart finds this a profoundly challenging view and one that in her opinion opens the Christian debate to new and exciting possibilities. Along with Graham Ward she agrees that Jesus' body witnesses to many displacements, that is, incarnation, circumcision, transfiguration and resurrection all profoundly destabilize our idea of what materiality really is. The church as the body of Christ shares in a very unstable body, a body that calls all knowledge about bodies into question. Stuart suggests that this also calls into question notions of gender as well. In addition, according to Stuart, Christians live in a world that they believe is in the process of redemption, and so they have to live in critical connection with social constructions. Therefore, Christians will not only perform gender differently but will also have radical views about beauty and perfect embodiment. Stuart reflects on the experience of some disabled people who have different ideas about body boundaries. Many who use wheelchairs claim there is an invisible boundary between them and the chair, and the same claim is made by those with artificial limbs. This body

---

20. Elisabeth Stuart, 'Disruptive Bodies: Disability, Embodiment and Sexuality', in Lisa Isherwood (ed.), *The Good News of the Body: Sexual Theology and Feminism* (Sheffield: Sheffield Academic Press, 2000).

boundary fluidity is, according to Stuart, a good model for Christ, who knows no fixed rules of matter and dissolves boundaries. Christians have had at the heart of their symbolic world a broken, tortured and displaced body, yet they have been slow to engage with this reality living, as they have done in the ivory tower of dualistic metaphysics. It will be very exciting to see what new and challenging face of Christ emerges as all of us overcome our fear and look in the face of the impaired Christ.

To Suffer or Not to Suffer...?

As we have seen, the idea of a suffering Christ has been problematic for women, and particularly those of colour, who have suffered double oppression as a result of such an image. However, as we have also come to expect, women's engagement with theological concepts transforms them through rooting them in the ground of experience and speaking them contextually and with compassion. In paying attention to a concept that has damaged women, feminist theologians are not only respecting the tradition but also acknowledging that, in ways that may not be obvious to contemporary women, the suffering Christ has been a source of strength to our foresisters. This simply highlights the fact the Christ is best understood contextually. The contextual Christ is a liberator, while the universal Christ cannot speak to all conditions.

While I am not suggesting that suffering and sacrifice are the same, I do think that the idea of a suffering Christ raises questions for our consumerist society. We see clearly how our appetite for 'things' causes the physical suffering and premature deaths of many of the world's inhabitants, but there is another side to this, which is our willingness to sacrifice comfort for justice. The western world has developed a very wide comfort zone around itself, and this is so entrenched that we believe it has to exist or we will be deprived. I feel sure that if governments started to trade fairly and slowly reduce our comfort zone, many of us would feel as though we were suffering. Is there a place for this in a Christian society? Yes, of course there is and the sooner the better. Theologizing this as mutual relation is perhaps a second step since people are slow to understand the benefits of such a way of living. However, stalwart self-sacrifice may just catch on!!

We live in a world that ignores the suffering of the majority (Third World) while ever striving for medical advances to eradicate the, at times, mere inconveniences of the minority. In the light of traditional theologies' glorification of suffering and feminist theologies' engagement with diversity and empowerment, how should we view our increasing drive to cure/prevent disabilities? What should we think about foetal tissue research? What sort of mindset is at work when we wish to eradicate, in the so-called First World, different types of embodiment? It appears that the mindset is a dualistic one with its notions of imperfection well in place. So should feminist theologians resist it? Can we really see ourselves arguing, indirectly at least, for the goods of suffering, which is an inevitable consequence of arguing for different embodiment? The medical future holds many challenges for feminist theology and we need to be as clear as we can about the value of the body and the diversity of experience through bodies. Suffering may be a concept we will have to rethink, since letting go of it altogether may usher in an almost unthinkable reality.

Chapter Six

Christ Sophia

As we have seen feminist theologians have engaged in creative theology in order to dislodge the most oppressive aspects of the Christ symbol. This task has called for hermeneutical skill, imagination and moral courage in addition to the unshakeable belief that a more inclusive and liberating symbol may emerge from the wreckage of the patriarchal mind set. No small test of faith! In their attempts to put a female face to Christ, some theologians have posited the Christa or Christa community, Edwina Sandys sculpted the first contemporary Christa, a female hanging on the cross, for the United Nations Year of Women in 1975. This image was greeted with both pleasure and disgust. Margaret Argyle created a tapestry, which she entitled 'The Bosnian Christa', and we are fortunate enough to have a copy at the institution where I work. The range of reactions has amazed me, and I am speechless at both the empowerment that women, particularly those who have suffered abuse, find by looking at the image and equally the venom that spews from those who find a crucified woman an inappropriate image as a Christian icon. The latter group consistently fail to see the pain and the cultural relevance. They condemn the image, seeing the physicality of it as a break with Christian tradition, and failing to grasp that the narrative is deeply Christian and simply transferred to an image that has poignancy in our time. Rita Brock, while sympathetic to Christas, prefers to think of Christa community, which she believes shifts the emphasis from Jesus the heroic redeemer to Christology as a community act. Indeed the community itself becomes the healing centre of the redemptive activity. Although Brock goes further than others in focusing on community in order to get away from hero worship, the notion of Christa does not seem far enough removed from Christ to avoid lapses into old bad habits. However, like the other models it has its place, and for many women it is a stepping-stone to totally new ways of imaging the divine.

Others prefer the notion of Sophia. However, before Christian theologians were directly using the notion of Sophia in their christological debates, such authors as Merlin Stone[1] were reclaiming her for the Goddess tradition. Her argument was that the earliest religious impulses of humans were directed towards female deities, and the people whose stories are told in biblical literature were no different in their inclinations toward the divine. She and others[2] suggest that the female divine was suppressed in biblical religion due to the over-emphasis of the male monotheistic God. This emphasis means that Sophia's role in creation (Prov. 8.22-31) is totally played down, and the question is not asked about her existence before Yahweh. We tend to forget that the world of antiquity understood the cosmos as a creating mother and so for them a female creator was quite natural. Sophia is always involved with the people and thrives in chaos, not wishing to set in place the numbing rigidity of the disembodied word. Sophia is referred to throughout the Hebrew Scriptures and is often viewed as the Queen of Heaven, who was, surprisingly, worshipped in the Temple of Solomon for hundreds of years. It is, then, not that Sophia, the female divine, never existed but rather that she was overcome by the agenda of patriarchal religion. While she is never fully vanquished, she is sidelined, and once the Christian story begins she is subsumed in the messianic imagery surrounding Jesus. This highlights the power of language, because when Sophia became Logos it was not just her gender that was changed, but rather the whole concept underpinning her was transformed through disembodiment and the imposition of absolutes. It is from this starting point that feminist theologians have attempted to uncover and reclaim the power of Sophia. As we shall see they do it in a variety of ways.

However, it also needs to be pointed out that recovering the symbol and placing it in a christological framework has its problems. There are some who are offended by such a practice because they cannot begin to imagine that the divine could be viewed as female, while others object that Sophia is a Jewish concept that should not be Christianized. This suggests anti-Semitism by default through simply assuming that the Jewish tradition was a precursor to Christianity and that all Jewish theology is up for theological colonization. This has been a tendency in feminist theology that is slowly being redressed (see Chapter 7). As we shall see, not all those who reclaim Sophia do so in such an insulting way.

1.   See Merlin Stone, *When God Was a Woman* (New York: Harvest; HBJ Books, 1976).
2.   See Raphael Patai, *The Hebrew Goddess* (New York: Avon Books, 1978); Asphodel Long, *In a Chariot Drawn by Lions* (London: Women's Press, 1991); Alix Pirani, *The Absent Mother: Restoring the Goddess to Judaism and Christianity* (London: Mandala, 1991).

Jesus: Sophia's Prophet

Elisabeth Schüssler-Fiorenza approaches feminist Christology in a slightly different way from many of her feminist sisters. She sets out to explore the theoretical frameworks of various discourses about Jesus and not to write revolutionary biography or a post-patriarchal Christology. Feminist movements seek to intervene in the struggle over the control and commodification of knowledge; they try to keep the knowledge of radical equality alive in the eyes of the disenfranchised. This is a hard struggle in the reality of global systems and requires global analysis. Fiorenza believes that theology has to play its part, or religion in general and Christology in particular will be a dangerous weapon in the hands of those who wish to reinstate conservative and oppressive regimes. Conservative political forces use religion as a cover for arguments that will lead to their advantage. Fundamentalists employ the modern media while rejecting many of the political and ethical values espoused by the modern democracy:

> The political-religious right claims the power to name and define the true nature of biblical religions against liberation theologies of all colors and geographical locations. Its well financed think tanks are supported by reactionary political and financial institutions that seek to defend kyriarchal capitalism.[3]

These right-wing groups have portrayed emancipated women as signifiers of western decadence or modern secular atheism and have also presented masculine power as divine power. In such a context women must not give up the power of naming by respecting conservative claims to ownership of the texts. Feminist theologians should seek to destabilize the centre by speaking both the language of our intellectual theological fathers and the dialects of our feminist sisters. Feminist theology is a political practice not only for personal change but also structural change. Because so many women collude with the structures, feminist theology has to address itself to tackling the self-hatred that so many women have as well as confronting cultural disrespect for women.

Fiorenza uses the term kyriarchy rather than patriarchy to describe the system as she sees it. This is because she thinks that 'the hermeneutical center of a critical feminist theology of liberation cannot simply be women'.[4] It has to account for other oppressions and for women as oppressor. The emperor/lord/master/father is the ruler and this legitimates the intellectual and cultural

---

3. Elisabeth Schüssler-Fiorenza, *Jesus: Miriam's Son, Sophia's Prophet* (New York: Continuum, 1994), p. 8.

4. Fiorenza, *Jesus*, p. 14.

framework that exerts social control. The Catholic Church and modern capitalism are modelled on classical kyriarchy, with a person at the top casting dictates at the lives of millions. This term kyriarchy comes from the Greek city-state where we see clearly the tensions between radical democratic ideas and the kyriarchical reality. It goes without saying that democracy is an illusion under such a system, although that illusion is tenderly nurtured, since it suits those in control to appear open to people-powered change!

Fiorenza is aware that most Christologies to date are in one way or another products of kyriarchal thinking. Liberal Enlightenment christologies have glorified this model, with the Jesus seen as the greatest man that ever lived, who is also defiant, autonomous and beyond all human limitations. This has in reality meant that we are under the spell of male white supremacy, because the white male is always cast as the hero in our culture, while Jesus himself has been somewhat bleached over the years and also appears as the white hero. It would appear beyond doubt that classical Christologies were shaped by imperial interests, and this can be illustrated by highlighting the words used in various christological definitions. For example, Chalcedon, which made its declaration in the name of the church fathers and the emperors Marcion and Valentinian, used two separate Greek words to describe incarnation. The one least used was *enanthropesin*, which means to live among or have human form. The one used the most was *oikonomia*, which means household management or law/order/administration. Therefore, the mystery of the incarnation in this usage is best described as mystery of the Lord's order/law/management/ economy. The mystery is that of kyriarchal power. This is further highlighted by all the exclusions that the Council proclaimed. The Council defined itself as the holder of power and meaning, of no less than divine power and meaning. The true nature of Jesus was defined as oikonomia and therefore confirmed the 'givenness' of the imperial order and intolerance of diversity. Thus Chalcedon was political.

Fiorenza uses the ekklesia of wo/men as a counter argument to kyriarchal definitions. (Wo/men to show we are not one group but fragmented by structures of class, race, etc.) To articulate ekklesia shows that an alternative system that is fully inclusive and just can be found. It also calls for the herme- neutic of suspicion as we try to assess 'the kyriarchal effects of Christological articulations on the lives of wo/men in the global village'.[5] This critique shows up kyriarchy and the politics of meaning. Fiorenza tries to engage with various christological discourses in order to intervene in and subvert the 'politics of

---

5. Fiorenza, *Jesus*, p. 30.

meaning'. She claims that the women's movement can offset the oppression of kyriarchal Christology by developing emancipatory praxis. When we are immersed in action we become able to subvert dominant meanings through face-to-face encounters. However, she warns that even a relational Christology, grounded as it is in action, should guard against being too personal. It still needs to be articulated in socio-political terms, because the modern liberation question is no longer does God exist but what kind of God are we proclaiming in a world of oppression. How does God liberate? Redemption for feminist theology is about liberation, and therefore it involves struggle against oppression as well as a struggle for personal integrity and human freedom; it is about wholeness and transformation. It is seen not just as personal journeys but is also about societal journeys, and about redeeming impoverished visions and healing a damaged planet. It is a totally inclusive concept, which requires that we see creation and redemption in positive relation to one another. Grey points out that for women this process of creation/redemption is crucial, that we have to really experience ourselves as 'good creation'. This is not that easy in a world that uses us as sexual objects; objects for violence; ornaments; money-making objects; and as people whose opinions are not easily valued. We all have to recover a sense of self-worth, because being redeemed in Christ is not enough.

Fiorenza's own approach is to search for divine wisdom, Sophia. This is a difficult task, since traces of her are buried in masculinist Christological traditions. Nor should we be lulled into thinking that, even if we find her, the lot of women will be improved. The Hebrew Scriptures make her more visible and are positive about her, but the lot of actual women was not always a happy one. The Christian Scriptures, particularly the Johannine literature, highlight a stage when Jesus is given the attributes of Sophia. Some of the earliest traditions of the Jesus movement understood Jesus as the prophet of Sophia who was to make the realm of God available to the poor and marginalized. As a child of Sophia he also made the message experientially available to all through ministry and miracles. One of the earliest Jesus sayings states that 'Sophia is justified by her children' (QLK7.35), which signifies that Sophia is with all her children and is made just in and by them. The statements that have been hijacked to proclaim Jesus' atoning death can be seen in a different light as confirming that Jesus was the prophet of Sophia, for example, 'Therefore also the Wisdom of God said "I will send them prophets and apostles, some of whom they will kill and persecute"'(Lk. 13.34). This suggests that the earliest reflections on the nature of Jesus were sophialogy not Christology. Fiorenza wants to argue that Jesus does not close the Sophia tradition by being the last and greatest, which is a contradiction of the tradition; but rather that he opens it yet further. He stands in a long line of Sophia prophets, both men and women, who have been killed for the message they bring. Their deaths were not willed by Sophia, indeed they are lamented (QLK13.34). This lamentation is not directed at all the Jews but just at the governing authorities. Thus sophialogy helps overcome the anti-Jewish tendencies inherent in traditional Christology.

Many scholars think that Jesus replaced Sophia, but according to Fiorenza close examination of the texts shows that Jesus is handed the attributes that Sophia always possessed (Mt. 11.25-27), therefore he received them from her. The Father God does give Jesus knowledge but Sophia, who was present at creation with Yahweh already, has the qualities that Jesus inherits from the father. Fiorenza explains the exclusive father/son language as the drawing of boundaries by the early communities. The baptism of Jesus confirms the view that he was a prophet of Sophia, as she descended upon him like a dove (the grey dove was the symbol of the immanent Sophia, whereas a turtle dove was a symbol of her transcendence: Philo). Like Sophia Jesus found no dwelling place among humans and so was given one in heaven (Sophia: *1 En.* 42.1-2; Sir. 24.3-7). Similarly, they were both exalted and enthroned, assuming rulership over the whole cosmos (Phil. 2.6-11; Isa. 45.23). The latter echoes the Isis cult, and so it is no surprise that Jesus too is called Lord, which was the title given to Isis. The Christ is understood in terms of Sophia as the mediator of the first creation and as the power of a new qualitatively different creation. It is this understanding of Sophia that allowed Christianity to have a cosmic agenda, to believe it could change the world.

She Who Is/or Is She?

Elisabeth Johnson also develops her Christology in terms of Jesus-Sophia. She is convinced that the early church used many of the traditions about personified Wisdom in order to come to an understanding of who Jesus was. Indeed, she asserts that it was only after he had become identified with wisdom that he was understood as the only begotten son. This signals a slight difference between the theories of Fiorenza and Johnson. Fiorenza, as we have seen, has no desire to view all the attributes of Jesus as the last word. For Johnson the identification of Jesus with personified wisdom does a number of things. It illustrates the importance of everyday living in the unfolding of the kingdom and it offers female metaphors as part of the divine process.[6] It also makes

6.   Elisabeth Johnson, 'Redeeming the Name of Christ', in Catherine Mowry LaCugna

inclusion the central element of salvation. That is to say, those who are normally excluded are counted as friends, accepted, sought after and loved not simply tolerated or worse still forgive. Jesus, as the child of Sophia, gives hope for the establishment of right relations across all boundaries.

For Johnson the stories of resurrection illustrate how Sophia rises again and again in unimaginable ways asserting that the gift of life cannot be overcome even by extreme torture and death. She will rise. The disciples are then commissioned to make the inclusive goodness of Sophia 'experientially available'.[7] It could be argued that Christianity is a resurrection faith only when this occurs. It is sadly true that Christianity has not always been concerned with spreading experiences of empowering goodness and inclusivity but has rather gloried in its own ability to define and therefore manipulate 'the Christ'. As Johnson points out, asserting that Sophia was in Jesus defuses any sexist claims as well as claims to religious exclusivism. Personified Wisdom is at work all over the world and in many different traditions and therefore Christianity can no longer claim special revelation. Sophia is also inherent in the world and so demands a far greater ecological awareness and striving for balance and right order in the natural world.

For Johnson, Sophia pitches her tent in the midst of the world and struggles for life. This has certain implications in relation to the maleness of Jesus which has been a hindrance for women. As Sophia the Christ allows women to rethink anthropology in an egalitarian way, since she is available to all and living in the midst of all. Johnson suggests we are able to celebrate one human nature and the interdependence of multiple differences. She claims this is not an argument for complementarity, but it appears to be dangerously close to it. Perhaps this closeness is assumed because she does not at any stage in her argument actually challenge the notion of gender performance and the relevance this has in the creation of our social worlds. Simply to celebrate difference is not so far from the papal position of 'different but equal', and most feminists have understood the agenda behind that approach and have not embraced it. Of course, Johnson is saying that the maleness of Jesus was important for him but it is not important for us. As true as this may be, it does not seems a strong enough statement in a gendered and sexist world and church where sex does matter.

This inclusive nature of Sophia can also be seen in the inclusive table community of Jesus. All the outcasts are gathered and called friends, thus

(ed.), *Freeing Theology: The Essentials of Theology in Feminist Perspective* (New York: Harper & Row, 1993), pp. 120-34 (122).

7.   Johnson, 'Redeeming the Name of Christ', p. 124.

releasing hope and an experience of liberation from social constraints; people are released from their social positions in to a new vision of relationality.[8] This, of course, proved far too challenging for the world in general and resulted in the death of Jesus. However, for Johnson the resurrection proves the enduring and renewing power of Sophia because she will always rise and renew the earth. In this way Sophia Christ signals the victory of Shalom through the power of compassion and not the sword. It is in this light that Johnson feels able to interpret the crucifixion as a struggle for new creation, one that evokes the rhythm of pregnancy, delivery and birth. There is some- thing very unsettling about this idea since it is able to contain a horrible act of public torture and death, with all the political implications that holds, within the act of birth. I am not sure that it captures the political nature of the death of Jesus, yet it could equally be argued that it politicizes the birth of children in an important and challenging way. While I do not think that this was Johnson's original intention it could be argued that each new birth, each new creation demands that the world be a better place, a place more able to embrace in justice and compassion this new incarnate Sophia.

Johnson argues that once the emphasis is removed from the once-and-for-all Christ, then the story of Christ Sophia has to include the story of those who were also engaged in the process. Many of these were women. In this way, then, the stories of women become part of the salvific narrative not as mere by-standers but as participants with Sophia. Not only were the women active in the life of Jesus but they continued the life of Sophia beyond his death. Mary Magdalene witnessed the resurrection and women were hubs of the early groups and they continued to be the embodiment of Sophia when the male disciples questioned the vision by running away and doubting. Women then remained the source of Sophia, they remained her faithful actors.

Johnson is able to extend the realm of Sophia to the earth itself, a theme she is able to pick up from the Hebrew Scriptures. The redeeming power of Sophia extends to the cosmos and draws people towards a more responsible and compassionate relation with the earth and all its non-humans inhabitants which leads us to discover that we are genetically closer to the rest of creation than our elitist anthropology has previously allowed us to imagine. This should worry us when we consider that apes are thought to be on a road to extinction, one forecast suggesting that they have 20 years at the most to survive. When will we understand that we are not immune to extinction and we are genetically vulnerable and in addition there is no saviour/Rambo miraculously to intervene.

8.   Johnson, *She Who Is*, p. 157.

In the face of her own arguments Johnson is mystified as to how the church has so successfully trivialized the doctrine of the incarnation. They have, she argues, reduced it to petty disputes about gender and human superiority all of which fall into insignificance next to a real understanding of the power of incarnation. The inner dynamic of incarnation speaks of bodiliness and the profound relatedness of all humans (and non-humans) in a passionate striving for liberation.[9] This liberation depends on both the universality of love and the particularity of love; the friendship of God, which pervades the cosmos nevertheless needs to be made manifest in acts of inclusion and justice making.

Johnson is clear that, while Sophia strives for the flourishing of the world and those who live in it, she is also radically distinct from the world. She remains always in her self yet her essence is relatedness. Johnson argues that this can be seen in the life of Jesus where Sophia is acting and animating and grounding him in relationality and community; yet she is not him, and her presence can disappear when relation is shattered. Johnson does not wish to lose the idea that God is also absolute mystery, unoriginated origin and goal of the universe. This is the point at which her thought sounds like the Catholic doctrine that formed her, and one wonders if the feminist agenda only runs as far as finding a female face to place on an otherwise unaltered body of theology. Perhaps this is a little too harsh, since we can see that Johnson does to some extent remould the Christological debate. However, there are dangers, and the joy of inclusion should not numb feminist theologians to the ever-lurking power of patriarchal discourses.

Christ: Woman in the Ghetto

Park Soon Kyung declares that Jesus is a symbolic female as he identifies with those who are hurt the most by society. In this context, then, he is a 'woman Messiah',[10] which is not unlike the black Christ put forward by womanist theologians. He becomes the one who, if he lived today, would be in the ghetto along with the lowest of the low. While the symbolism of this is very powerful there could be a danger that people will begin to compete to see who is so lowly in society that Jesus would be bound to live among them. This is not meant as a flippant point but merely to illustrate that there are dangers in viewing Jesus simply as the one who dwells with the dispossessed thereby giving them 'status'. What happens if their position changes to one of relative affluence or if they are in some small part caught up in the web of exploitation,

---

9. Johnson, *She Who Is*, p. 168.
10. Quoted in Chung, *Struggle*, p. 65.

on the side of gain, that advanced capitalism makes it so hard to avoid? Where is Christ then? However, it has to be admitted that when people are totally dispossessed and marginalized the symbol of Jesus with them in their suffering is a powerful one. The danger I feel lies in thinking that this is where one has to stay in order to remain with Christ. The question is raised as to whether Christ is most powerful among the poor and lowly and therefore what his place and power is among the less oppressed. Clearly, if he is only ever imaged as powerful when he is a marginalized victim there can be no place. This seems a logical, but unsatisfactory, conclusion of claiming Christ for the lowly.

Perhaps it is a situation that Christ Sophia overcomes, since this understanding of Christ enables us to understand the power of Sophia available to all. In prioritizing the poor, there is no idea that Christ only dwells with the poor, and so indeed if one is no longer poor Sophia may still guide actions and lifestyle. The poor then become a group who act as moral judges of the not poor in that their conditions in life demand that capital be generated in a just and equal way. I think that a feminist Christ for the not poor has not yet been worked out but is desperately needed, not to sooth the conscience of the vast majority of feminist theologians who can no longer claim to be dispossessed or poor but in order to understand more fully the nature of that which we call divine.

The Wisdom of Fools

Mary Grey[11] also engages with Sophia in the hope of finding revelation for today. She sets out a dialogue between two myths, those of Logos and Sophia. The former is shown to create a high-tech and disembodied rule-driven world of universal 'executives', while the latter is 'a dark haired woman telling stories by (…)glowing embers'.[12] Her tales are of freedom and courage, and she responds to loneliness and despair with tales of hope. When Logos holds a press conference about world progress Sophia interrupts and puts the case for those who move at a different pace, declaring that women and children suffer for this so-called progress. Logos asserts reason over feeling as the way ahead!

Grey presents us with a compelling picture that speaks from deep mythological roots yet addresses the issues of today. She appeals for Sophia to be central to decision-making processes within and outside the churches, since the Logos Christ simply reinvents the mistakes of the past by re-entrenching

---

11.   Mary Grey, *The Wisdom of Fools? Seeking Revelation for Today* (London: SPCK, 1993).
12.   Grey, *The Wisdom of Fools?*, p. 7

hard cold logic over the lived experiences of women and men. How are we to understand the revelation of God since for Grey the Logos inhibits that knowing. She is not the first to suggest that we know in and through our bodies in a far more urgent and meaningful way than we do through logic and doctrines. God, then, it could be argued will not shine in the new millennium through the face of the calculated Logos of cold disembodied metaphysics but will move amidst the story tellers at the hearth of reality and in the lives of women and men.

So what is it that Sophia is declaring? She is shouting 'epiphanies of connection' in a broken world. Sophia not only highlights the connections between people and the planet but also makes plain the ethical implications and empowers the action. For Grey the power of connection and commitment in relationship calls into question any notion of divinely given destiny. She sees these ideas as fundamentally incompatible, and so, by implication, is questioning the entire Christian scheme of salvation. It becomes a far more open-ended affair with no guarantees and no heroes. There can be no conformity to a rigid set of rules laid down by the Logos as part of the great Master Plan; there is instead an imaginative embrace of the world and a celebration of the diversity of connection. Like others before her Grey declares that the profound nature of incarnation is limited by restricting it to the person of Jesus. Sophia moves far beyond this and into the most unlikely places in order to highlight the awesome power of incarnation.

In addition Sophia breaks the silences on which patriarchal abuse has thrived. In moving beyond narrow definitions she allows all people to speak from their experience and enables people to hear. We come to realize our common stories and to find strength in that as well as to hear the pain and difference of others. There is power in the breaking of the silence. Grey says of Sophia:

> She is hope for the marginalized community because, as epiphany of prophetic-mystic community, she is the revelation for today that the long exile and waiting is over, new voices are heard in the wilderness, and women may safely leave the desert and be the leaven for beloved community'.[13]

These words are inspiring, but they may be useless if they are not rooted in something more concrete than simply wishing it to be the case. Grey encourages us by imaging Sophia as practical wisdom, which addresses structural problems with solid actions. Protests, just weekly shopping and vigils are all signs that Sophia is spinning her web of creative alternatives. Sophia is praxis

---

13. Grey, *The Wisdom of Fools?*, p. 143.

and this makes a difference in the world and should empower believers when they grasp that Jesus was not the only incarnation of Sophia.

Grey shows clearly that simply feminizing the divine will not move us forward, and so she offers us Sophia, who stands in stark contrast to Jesus Logos. Nothing will change if we continue to assume that Logos is a neutral and harmless concept, for it is in fact the underpinning logic of much of the worst in the world. Was Jesus of Nazareth such a person? We have no way of knowing. What we do know is that under the guidance of the power brokers of Christianity this is who he has become and in so doing he has been rendered useless as a saviour in our present world. The time has come for a shift, and Grey and others advocate an embrace of Sophia, an embrace of the feeling, passionate, wise face of the divine, an embrace that will melt frozen hearts and let incarnation flow.

Eco-Sophia

Celia Deane-Drummond[14] attempts to claim Sophia as a more positive ecotheological image than Gaia as used by Ruether and others. She reminds us that it has ancient roots with Aristotle seeking Sophia as a bridge between scientific knowledge and intuitive reason and a path to the highest things in nature. He thought that the things that flowed from Sophia were theological but were known as scientific elements. As we know, Aristotle, through the fathers, had a profound affect on Christian theology, and Deane-Drummond believes this is still a concept that can yield invaluable theological treasure.

She asserts that the feminist use of wisdom starts from experience in the world rather than from wisdom as a theological concept as found in the fathers. (She reflects a great deal upon the orthodox use of Sophia, but the detail of her argument is not relevant here.) She claims that there is very little difference in the way the concept is used apart from the fact that for the men it emanates from above and for feminists wisdom is found in the very stuff of life. Deane-Drummond is claiming that love and entreaty are the same regardless of the direction from which they emerge. There seems to be a fundamental misunderstanding of the arguments put forward by feminists in relation to the dangers of dualism, for it is precisely the splitting of concepts from the root bed of experience that can, and does, lead to power and abuse.

---

14. Celia Deane-Drummond, 'Sophia: The Feminine Face of God as a Metaphor for an Ecotheology', in *Feminist Theology No. 16* (Sheffield: Sheffield Academic Press, 1997), pp. 11-31.

Love looks very different depending on who is defining it. Dualistic metaphysics are not neutral and they have, historically, hurt women.

However, following Deane-Drummond's argument, we find that she picks up on the notion of emancipatory wisdom as put forward by Catherine Keller. This wisdom can incorporate both the academic and the ecclesiastical worlds that call it to account. She claims that it lets things become and is linked to principles of social change in favour of the vulnerable in the community. Wisdom, for Keller, signals a move from orthodoxy to orthopractice. This approach and that of Moltmann-Wendel, who sees wisdom as earthy, imaginative and passionate, is a good starting ground for Deane-Drummond and her ideas around Sophia as a positive ecotheological model. She is, however, cautious since she feels that Moltmann-Wendel is too positive about the earthy and rather stereotypical in relation to women. Nevertheless, the active and passionate role of wisdom leads her to suggest that there is a clear eschatological goal towards which the whole of creation conspires, and women and men aid this conspiracy through making correct choices about the environment.[15]

Deane-Drummond utilises the work of Elisabeth Johnson, Claudia Camp and Mary Grey in order to provide the foundations of her argument. Through a review of their work she is able to show how wisdom has deep biblical roots and how it is revelatory and cosmic. Once this has been established, she applies her findings to ecotheology. She asserts that wisdom provides the link between the sacred and the secular and demands that we reject all knowing that is against the commandments of God. She is, then, highlighting that there is a juridical role in wisdom that must not get lost in the natural realm of theologies of creation. In addition she also wishes to keep a transcendent element to God which she fears other ecotheologies put to one side. In Sophia, Deane-Drummond finds the way in which God and the world become linked yet not one. This wisdom has two faces, that of the natural wisdom of ecology and that of cultural wisdom found in the Scriptures. While insisting that the distinction is not a sharp one, she claims it is there. She calls for ecotheology to include the historical sphere and not simply to exist as a backdrop to human history.

Deane-Drummond also emphasizes the place of the cross in an ecotheology of wisdom. Picking up on an Orthodox theologian who claims that wisdom has a shadow side which faces evil in the world, she claims that the cross becomes the wisdom of the Christian Scriptures. It is through this event that creation and redemption are brought together in a single theme: 'Once the Wisdom of all creation is seen as caught up in the Wisdom of God as expressed

15. Deane-Drummond, 'Sophia', p. 20.

in the cross, the cross becomes the place of crucifixion of all of creation, not just suffering humanity'.[16]

There is a solidarity in suffering that Deane-Drummond wishes to declare as being in some way salvific. In addition Sophia as Mother encourages us to see that wisdom gives birth to the earth and to add a corrective to the notion of God as Father. Deane-Drummond believes that she shows how the idea of wisdom retains notions of transcendence while also 'softening' the harshness of a male God and stressing the relevance of wisdom for ecotheology. What she sees as a holistic approach is really little more than quite traditional theology with a pinch of Sophia to add spice. This is not entirely surprising, since she relies heavily on Elisabeth Johnson, who, as we have seen, resurrects Sophia but never quite pushes the feminist agenda to its passionate conclusion. Deane-Drummond offers a way in which those who wish to speak the new language may do so without too much cost to themselves.

Beware the Female Divine!

There can be little doubt that women need to reawaken the long-slumbering traditions associated with the female divine, and the reasons for this were discussed and established many years ago by Carol Christ.[17] Although she was talking primarily about the Goddess, the same arguments apply and, of course, the same reservations to the argument. Religious symbols that simply focus on the male give the impression that women's power can never be legitimate or beneficial. Indeed, Christian history is littered with the bodies of women thought to be too powerful and therefore dangerous. If we can ensure through the embrace of female symbols that this scapegoating stops then we have much to celebrate in the notion of Christ Sophia. Christianity has traditionally feared the power of the female body and has attempted to control it. In Christ Sophia we see a fully embodied face of the divine and this leaves room for women to re-establish their own embodied divinity. In so doing many things are challenged from religious taboos to cultural denigrations of the female body. Women are able to call for embodied justice, which ranges from respect and dignity of childbirth to safety on the streets and in the home. Christ Sophia allows women to include their bodies in the theological discourse. Of course, there is a danger here that has to be guarded against, which is that

16.   Deane-Drummond, 'Sophia', p. 29.

17.   See Carol Christ, 'Why Women Need the Goddess: Phenomenological, Psychological and Political Reflections', in Carol Christ and Judith Plaskow (eds.), *Womanspirit Rising* (San Francisco: Harper & Row, 1979), pp. 273-87.

women become totally associated with child-bearing and fecundity. These have been negative associations in the past and while women would not wish to deny them, they would also not wish to be wholly identified with them.

Carol Christ identifies the Goddess as being able to legitimize the female will, and this can also be said of Christ Sophia. While Sophia is embedded in the stuff of life, it is the will of those who wish to embody her that is of use in the world. Self-affirmation and community direction are seen as positive aspects of any prophet of Sophia, unlike any follower of the traditional Christ. Traditional Christianity has emphasized the negation of self and the gift of one's will to God. Christ Sophia needs focused and powerfully willed people in order to enact the redeeming vision. An engagement with Christ Sophia offers women the opportunity to assert their wills but it also offers ways to do this that are non-patriarchal. In addition Christ Sophia places women back in the Christian story. Patriarchal and hierarchical readings do not allow for women to see their constructive place in the life of Jesus and as such they have been excluded from church and society. Acknowledging that it is Christ Sophia who we see among Jesus and those he engaged with allows a whole new reading and one that empowers women; we reclaim our history and with it a sense that we are people who make a difference. While there are many similar arguments that can be used both by those who wish to assert the divine as Goddess or as Christ Sophia, we should not lose sight of the fact that Christian theologians are not claiming Goddess status for Sophia. Whether this is a good or bad thing is for the reader to decide!

There are further advantages in resurrecting the Sophia tradition, since wisdom can be shown to engage with matters of feminist concern. The Christ Sophia is inclusive, strives for justice and is empowering. In addition the notion of atonement can be removed, and this notion, as we have seen, has worked against women. Schüssler-Fiorenza argues for Sophia from the Q material, a body of material that has no Passion narratives, and thus women can engage with the death of Jesus in a more empowering way and not be guided to limited and devastating interpretations.

There has been criticism from those who insist the work of salvation has to have a clear and usable 'narrative'. That is to say, if we fix on Jesus as *the* saviour, then we have a life story and sets of circumstances to reflect upon and develop a Christian life from. However, if we have wisdom, moving as she will and leading all kinds of people into salvific paths the story gets muddied. Where is the clear narrative with beginning, middle and end? Well, there is not one and that is just the point. The Sophia tradition opens up the redemptive possibilities and throws responsibility on our shoulders so there are no guarantees but a greater range of salvific potential and possibilities.

Chapter Seven

The Feminist Future:
Jesus Christ or Sophia's Empowered Daughters?

Under the weight of feminist analysis the Christ of metaphysical absolutes is being exposed to the lived experience of women and men, and is crumbling. It is true that many faces of Christ are emerging, and it can be argued that this is precisely what we witness in the gospel reflections on the meaning of Jesus. There we find that we are presented with statements of meaning rather than factual accounts, and so we see very little of Jesus of Nazareth, but we are engaged with emerging Christic narratives.

As Daphne Hampson has pointed out, if we remain focused on the Jesus of history we cannot move forward, and indeed, Christianity that focuses in this way may not be able to address the increasingly complex moral questions that are emerging in our world. Fortunately, the gospel writers present us with reflections on praxis rather than documents proclaiming orthodoxy. Indeed, the gospel writers appear to have shown no fear regarding adaptation of material, and they illustrate how the ongoing narrative of faith cannot be polluted by having communal experience enter into it. We have known for quite some time that we are less than honest if we attempt to construct one pure and uninterrupted story about the life of Jesus because this is just not what the gospel record provides us with.

The Gospels provide us with a narrative, one that engages the life of Jesus in the ongoing story of Emmanuel, God with us, and the history of the Jewish people. What was unshakeable for them was the belief that God walked with them in their everyday lives and was on their side; that is to say, he was a God who had brought them out of bondage and made them a chosen people. Jesus was certainly part of that narrative but not the whole story; he was incorporated into a life of faith and expanded as the narrative itself expanded. To a certain extent the gospel writers were narrating the life and needs of their community through the life of Jesus. Sadly, Christian interpretation has fossilized a powerful and ongoing story into the narrow events of one life, that of Jesus of Nazareth. The main result of this approach has been that a select few have been the ones controlling the narrative, which they have, with amazing skill, turned into a Grand Narrative from which they have benefited. Feminist theology has once more engaged with the ongoing narrative of 'God with us' by inserting the stories of the silenced and marginalized into the unfolding of the story. Those who wish to maintain the status quo have declared this un-Christian. In fact it is a return to the gospel way of understanding the Christ; it is a commitment to expanding the narrative through praxis, and, equally, of expanding the praxis through the narrative.

The place of the narrative is crucial as it allows space to make real another reality. The lives of those who journeyed with Jesus were as unsettled and filled with questions of oppression and liberation as ours are today. Rather than live according to the reducing and depressing realities of their day they lived as though another reality were possible and in fact already present. They looked beyond the edges of their reality to another way of being, to the kingdom. Their narrative heritage played a huge part in this being possible as they lived in a world that knew the Messiah would come and that expected this event to overturn all oppressive regimes. Their engagement with this narrative was so intimate that they were able to live as though it were already the case.

How then can feminist theologians live as though the kingdom were already here? What should and could our relationship be with the ongoing narrative? What questions do we have to ask of the Christological discourse? What is positive about the emerging discourse that can carry us some way forward?

Jesus the Jew versus Christ the Anti-Semite.

One question that desperately needs addressing is that of Christian anti-Semitism, which is always a real danger when dealing with Christology. Despite all that we have known about methods of biblical interpretation and the folly of holding too fast to heroic tales, we have been slow to apply the knowledge. This has led to many kinds of 'false reading', some of which have had devastating effects. Jewish feminists have for some time been unhappy with the way in which some Christian feminists have uncritically continued to present Jesus as the saviour of women in first-century Palestine. Rather than move the Christian discourse away from its historic anti-Semitism much feminist theology has reinstated the problems.

The so-called 'teaching of contempt'[1] has its roots in the Christian distortion of Judaism, a distortion that portrays Jewish ideals as antithetical to Christian ideals. This has led to a scapegoating of Jews that in its secular form, led to most probably the worst abuses of the twentieth-century, the Holocaust. Feminist theologians have not always learnt from the mistakes of the past and have added another reason for seeing Judaism as inferior: it killed the Goddess and invented patriarchy. Yahweh is generally portrayed as the enemy of feminist values, while Jesus is their champion. The God of the Hebrew Scriptures is shown to be a male militarist and therefore as non-feminist. However, Von Kellenbach shows that Ruether and others will point to Near Eastern Goddess who is warlike and suggest that this is good for women. If this is true there is clearly a double standard here.

Christian theologians, even feminists, have suggested that the history of Israel is one of failures leading to the biggest failure of all, the murder of the Son of God. While I agree that Jewish history has not always been viewed positively, it really is pushing the point to suggest that feminist theologians would assert that Jews killed the Son of God. This does not figure in the Christology, which, as we have seen, does not understand the death of Jesus as anything other than political and therefore not as some kind of blasphemous rejection by infidels. Jesus was a Jew and was therefore caught up in the Jewish and Roman politics of the time; this was fact and should not be made into theological ammunition.

It does appear to be the case that some feminist theologians are suggesting, perhaps unwittingly, that Judaism gave birth to patriarchy and alone killed the Goddess. However, more nuanced writers are quite clear that this is not the case. Ruether explains how the male myth took the driving seat over Goddess myths in many Near Eastern cultures, not just the Israelite culture, while authors like Asphodel Long show how the Goddess was never fully eradicated from Judaism, as she was not from other Near Eastern cultures. While I agree that we have to be careful about the way in which certain ideas are put over, it is also a mistake to assume that a put down is meant. It appears to be true that Judaism embraced patriarchy, and this meant that the Goddess went underground, but this is far from suggesting that Judaism invented patriarchy and killed the Goddess.

Of course, the mistake that we have all made, I am sure, is to imply that Judaism is in some way a prologue for Christianity and therefore ceases to be

---

1. Katharina Von Kellenbach, 'Overcoming the Teaching of Contempt', in Athalya Brenner and Carole Fontaine (eds.), *A Feminist Companion to Reading the Bible: Approaches, Methods and Strategies* (Sheffield: Sheffield Academic Press, 1997), pp. 41-53.

truly valid in the present day. Worse still that as Christian feminists we can somehow take the bits from the Hebrew Scriptures that suit our arguments and interpret them completely in our own context, not paying attention to their historic and cultural roots. Appropriation works towards the elimination of difference and is essentially a non-feminist activity, but it is something that feminists do. Equally worrying is the way in which some feminists develop a hierarchy of oppression and place anti-Semitism on the list below sexism. It is regrettable, yet understandable, that such ways of thinking would develop. Understandable only because the ways of oppression are so many that one can feel overwhelmed if all are faced at one time, and this ends in list mentality whereby we try and decide what needs tackling first. However, the compilation of the lists says more about the person than about the need. Thankfully, there is increasing feminist awareness that all oppression is linked and while it is not possible to make lists, it is necessary to prioritize one's own action. This is a very different matter from list-making and should not be understood as exclusion or apportioning merit to one cause over another. There could be no excuse today for Mary Daly or any other feminist theologian to suggest that sexism is more important than the Holocaust.[2]

It goes without saying that Christian feminist theology needs to help forge respect for Jews and Judaism and that this is done best by giving up ideas of superiority and notions of 'correct readings' when it comes to shared texts like the Hebrew Scriptures. This does not mean that any critical engagement has to be shelved in favour of political correctness, but it does mean that Christian feminists need to be sure that this is scholarly and not a mere reinvention of centuries of anti-Semitism. Where does this leave us with Christology, a branch of theology that by its very nature appears to have to give unique status to Jesus? Do we have to imply that Jesus overcame all the shortcomings of Judaism, if we are to continue any christological discourse at all? Of course we do if we are going to continue to assert some metaphysical truths about the man. However, if we assume that Christ is an ethical construct, we do move a little further away from condemnation but are not entirely clear of it. After all we could still declare that Jesus was ethically superior to anything known by Judaism, but this of course is not the case since he owed his ethical and messianic understandings to his own Jewish background. In dispensing with the metaphysical nature of Christ, we are also able to ground Jesus more fully in his heritage by doing away with the kind of superman notions that he could miraculously become a man beyond his time, an eternal figure with a clear

2. She suggested this in 1978 in *Gyn/Ecology* (Boston: Beacon Press, 1978), in a discussion about shrinking feminist agendas to localized concerns.

view of ethical vistas. He was a man from his tradition. This, of course, means that we should become well acquainted with that tradition if we are to base our own understandings of the divine upon it. Rather than distance ourselves from it as some kind of outdated antiquity, it should be alive to us as we try to understand the immensity of incarnation, which sprang from the tradition. If we keep insisting on imposing Greek metaphysics on a tradition that was far more earthy, we will continue to have conflict, and so I suggest that one step towards addressing Christian anti-Semitism is to give up such an alien world view and begin to contemplate God with us (Emmanuel), the God of the Jews.

Jesus the Native[3]

As the colonial Christ fades into the sunset many new faces emerge but they are not alone, that is to say, they come with cultural heritages that have been subsumed under the weight of imperial cultures. This brings many exciting challenges for Christology because it is exposed to other ways of thinking. Christ can no longer find safety in Greek metaphysics since this concept is now examined by widely differing mindsets. For example, Aboriginal peoples have a totally different worldview from that of the Europeans who invaded them. The latter attempted over generations to eradicate the indigenous worldview and impose the one that fitted best with their concerns and ambitions, which, happened to be Christian. These days indigenous culture is reasserting itself and it poses interesting questions for Christology.

How is Christ the Lord to appear to cultures that are not organized along such hierarchical lines? Indeed, what Christ will emerge from such cultures? Further, land and belonging to it is of central importance to Aboriginal culture, and this is in stark contrast to a timeless and placeless Christ who hovers over all eternity. For Aboriginal people eternity is in the Dreaming, which is both in the past and in the present. It lays down the way that life is and determines patterns of behaviour. The Dreaming also grounds that which is divine in the here and now not in some transcendent realm. The divine is immanent in the land and in the Dreaming. What does all this say to Christology? Certainly there is no concept of incarnation that can be tied into Aboriginal culture and so Jesus becomes a dreaming hero, one who demands that people be rooted in their land. A figure found in the past and grounding

---

3.   See Kwok Pui-Lan, 'Jesus the Native', in Fernando F. Segovia and Mary Ann Tolbert (eds.), *Teaching the Bible: The Discourse and Politics of Biblical Pedagogy* (Maryknoll, NY: Orbis Books, 1998), pp. 69-85.

people in the present with little regard for the future, except in as far as it is the time of 'nows'. Is Christ transformed under such a worldview, and where are the eschatological promises?

Kwok Pui-Lan alerts us to other problems in relation to the way the Bible is read and the conclusions that are then reached. She states that we are taught to read with European eyes and thus the Christ who emerges still has a European feel to him. She is not at all surprised by this since she understands the quest for the historical Jesus as setting the scene for control of knowledge; just as westerners of the day went in search of the authentic 'native' so they went in search of the authentic Jesus, in order to own and control both.[4] This quest for origins was not a neutral academic exercise but was part of the justification of western superiority; in creating a mythic origin and claiming it as one's own, it is easy to avoid all the hard questions about real origins and simply to project one's own culture as pure and superior. In addition, if one claimed that one's own origins could be 'scientifically' proven while the origins of other cultures lay in myth and superstition, this was further evidence of superiority. Kwok does not consider it to be an accident that in the United States there was renewal of the search for the historical Jesus during the Reagan–Bush era, a time of political conservatism. While the first quest grew during time of colonial expansion, the second, she argues, grew when questions of immigration and national identity were hot political questions. Once again white would-be rulers used the christological discourse to assert their own uniqueness and dominance.

Kwok calls for a demystification of the master and argues that this cannot take place from within the discourse.[5] However, she also alerts us to the dangers of modern-day 'natives' assuming a privileged position in relation to text and interpretation. She calls for multiple frameworks and hermeneutical tools in order to spread the discourse as wide as possible and break down the narrow grip of western readings. There are many kinds of 'natives' and all should read and proclaim. In seeing only the poor or the indigenous as privileged in terms of understanding the real message of Christ, we are once again setting the west apart and giving it priority, since it is too advanced to be able to really understand a native like Jesus! Kwok wishes to claim native status for us all and encourage us to read through the lenses of gender, class, race, sexual orientation, age, disability and ethnic origin. In this way we are, and are not, native.

4.   Kwok, 'Jesus the Native', p. 77.
5.   Kwok, 'Jesus the Native', p. 80.

Jesus the native presents feminist theology with yet another challenge, which is how to move beyond Eurocentric methods without patronizing any particular group. The answer does not entirely lie in beginning from experience, because once experience is theorized the methods are once again western. Indeed, the constructs themselves are western, such as time and dualism. Many of the feminist interpretations of Christ that this book has highlighted have not broken beyond the western mind set despite being other than western in origin. This is not to criticize them but to illustrate how difficult it is to exorcize ingrained modes of thinking. Not only that, it is a relatively short space of time since alternate readings have had a voice, and we have to expect that the full impact of such liberation will take time to flourish.

Having highlighted some of the difficulties that face feminist theologians in their christological work, I am nevertheless encouraged to suggest some ways ahead. Naturally they are not to be understood as definitive or indeed as much more than the musings of a white, middle-class academic—limited in the extreme then! However, from where I stand they are questions to be engaged with in the hope of broadening the christological discourse.

The Flesh Becomes Word.

Feminist theologians have engaged with bodies and celebrate the fact that Jesus was portrayed as a very earthy man, sharing touch, engaging with nature, making strong political statements through the symbolic use of food and using fluid from his body to heal. (Both during the 'last supper' and in the feedings of thousands Jesus enacted shared power and the interconnected nature of flourishing; when each gives and receives there is more than enough and all are empowered through the equality of give and take. The actions that are now eucharistic are also powerful political symbols since all receive equally in cultures where inequality of access to food and wealth are blatantly obvious.) He appears to be a man who understood the importance of engaging the body in the struggle for liberation. What does feminist Christology learn from this?

The answer in part seems to be rooting deep, grounding in our world and our selves and bursting forth from the passion we find within. Heyward has developed the idea of dunamis and erotic connection and this seems to be one way ahead. One way in which Christ explodes into the reality of everyday life in an intimate and transforming way is through touch which is simple yet powerfully frightening. The power of touch, as witnessed in the life of Jesus and others, has been forgotten. Perhaps because the church fathers could only focus on the negative power of touch and laid such strong prohibitions against it and so we have forgotten how to do it. Christ is no longer linked to historical facts and so becomes the Christ of magical engagement rooted in the unfolding history of intimacy and empowerment. This Christ is the one who knew the power of touch to heal or to destroy and understood that the kingdom rests on the way in which we choose to touch each other and the world.

Christ, then, enables the flesh to become word and is not *The Word* made flesh. The colonization of Sophia (wisdom) into Logos (word) by the Christian tradition was a regrettable step. Not only did it deny the divine a female face but it also made very 'heady' a reality that was embodied. Divine wisdom as understood in the Hebrew Scriptures was active among the people walking in the market place and connecting people with the earth and everyday concerns. She was understood as the divine who led people to wisdom through rooting and grounding in themselves and their cultures. The women and men who followed her were often accused of being sexually immoral because of their sensual connection with creation in the pursuit of wisdom. However, this is best understood as exaggeration on the part of those who would prefer a more rigid and hierarchical system of belief, the priestly caste. Unfortunately for them those who find their truth through embodiment cannot be easily controlled. The wisdom that we gain through our bodies goes far deeper and convinces us to a greater extent than that found in our heads alone.

Feminist theology, by placing experience as the starting point of theological reflection, moves us back to our bodies. The body, far from being seen as sinful flesh and the site of all evil has emerged as a place of revelation and moral imperatives. The broken, bleeding and oppressed bodies of people demand that reality is changed and that they are made whole again—in this world. In this way, then, the flesh is speaking and being heard as a site of positive theological significance.

Indeed, there would be nothing of consequence being said if this explosive Christ simply appeared as a separate entity and consoled the downtrodden. It is the embodied power in all creation that makes the Christ a transforming reality. The flesh made word enables us to find a voice and to make our desires known. There are any number of examples of how this vision transforms the landscape of our lives: those who are starving present themselves as moral imperatives for the rest of us, and those who are poisoned by toxic waste challenge the ethics of business and profit, while those who labour under the genocidal reality of advanced capitalism present their bodies as a moral challenge to the Christian world. When the flesh is word there can be no talk of reward in heaven, for the bodies of these people are their heaven or hell and they will not wait and be soothed by pious utterances. The flesh enables Sophia (wisdom) to find creative alternatives.

The flesh as word also demands that absolutes be placed to one side and that listening take the place of unilateral dictation. Reality is constantly changing and what is required is the liberation of empowered speech and hearing not the misplaced confidence of eternal answers. The flesh has been silenced by metaphysics, hierarchy and once and for all incarnation. The narrative Christ speaks through the whole body and not just from the head, and it is this voice that returns power to people. The tower of Babel is an interesting example of how understanding is impaired by hierarchy: we do not hear so well at a distance, particularly when that distance is 'up'. The narrative Christ who is at the centre of creation translates the babble through engaging us in commitment to one another. This Christ illuminates the landscape through the power of intimate connection. Of course, the fact that we hear and see does not guarantee that we will achieve the required outcome but it does commit us to the struggle. By taking the flesh seriously, we open up a whole new landscape that has previously been veiled in distrust and 'original sin'. We open ourselves to the transforming power of incarnation.

A Christology of Risk

Moving, as I wish to do, from the once and for all Son of God to a more free-flowing Christ is a risky business. After all, this notion implies that Christ is only a possibility and not a guarantee. We place more at risk than salvation, but I think we also make the coming of the kingdom a more urgent requirement and, strangely, more attainable. In other words I am willing to sacrifice salvation, for liberation and the kingdom! I am taking salvation to have the more personalized meaning that it has had over the centuries and has today in evangelical quarters. This personal relationship with the saviour of the world, leading to individual salvation, is one that I wish to question in pursuit of a liberative Christology.

I believe a Christology of risk is perfectly in line with a religion that has incarnation at the heart. Becoming flesh is risky because it leaves behind all the certainty of metaphysical absolutes. Both the stories of the creation of the world and the crucifixion of Jesus highlight the point that nothing is guaranteed once we commit to life. The freedom required for the diverse wonder of creation to manifest is a huge risk. The God that Christians proclaim did take that risk in creation and even in incarnation, since the story maintains a degree of free will on the part of Jesus, thus keeping the redemptive tension. From a traditional point of view we can even say that God took the risk of redeeming a world that did not want it with a son who had the ability to run away. God took the risk of leaping into flesh, yet we have been encouraged to resist our enfleshment. In short, we have not dared to risk our own divine incarnation.

A Christology of risk means that the kingdom is always on a knife edge between the gloriously successful empowerment of ourselves and others, the devastatingly wrong and the mundanely unimaginative, imagination being, of course, a key point in our risk taking. If we are to break out of the hold that oppressive systems increasingly seem to have on the world, then vision empowered by imagination is crucial. We have to live as though the kingdom were already here, live counter culturally, live transgressively. Indeed, we have to incarnate the transgressive Christ, the one who plays with existing categories and breaks boundaries, the aim being a freer and more creative space for all in which aspects of incarnation not yet thought of can take root. By limiting our Christology to Jesus, we are in danger of reliving his limitations and prejudices. An unbiased reading of the gospels show that he appeared to have some that were embedded in his world. The woman with the haemorrhage is just one example that illustrates that Jesus may have allowed his own power of connection to be limited by his cultural surroundings and he had to be carried forward to break boundaries by the touch of another. The erotic, transgressive Christ spurs us on to be limitless and without boundary. This requires that we face imaginatively those boundaries erected in our own minds, cultures, religious systems and environments and overcome them through the power of intimate connection.

This is not an argument for an evolutionary view of Christ as we find in Teilhard de Chardin with his concept of the Omega Point. Although this idea allows for movement, it fails to take the ultimate step in the direction of risk by saying there is no fixed end point, that what we face is an open future spreading as it does into eternity. We are truly in the process and are co-creators and, (or not) co-redeemers with the Christ. We are in a real sense walking by faith in a resurrection hope, that is to say, we cannot be sure of our Christic power triumphing in the end but we are committed to transgressive rebellion that will change everyday life for ourselves and others. This process is never finished and is always fragile and partial.

It is important to stress that the whole of creation is involved in this process of Christic becoming so no human hierarchy can be set in place. Of course, we are also challenged to a new and dynamic view of our co-redeeming nature one that bends previously held systems. Perhaps we will see with scientific eyes the epiphanic organic Christ that Kwok Pui-Lan puts forward. The

Christ who erupts in many guises and often in the fabric of creation. The risky Christ, the Christ that does not have to be, yet time and again is.

Feminist Theology and the Power of Christ

Feminist theology has, to date, had trouble with notions of power. As we have seen even christological power is viewed by some as problematic. Hampson reminds us that power and autonomy require a great deal of negotiation if the latter is not to be totally consumed by the former. Simply because power is perceived as divine, it does not mean it is non-oppressive. If nothing else I hope this book has shown that.

How then are we to understand the power of Christ? It is no longer possible to say that the power of Christ lies in the heavens and intervenes to make all things well, at the end of time, if not now. The patriarchal imposition of power-over has caused suffering the world over, and it is this application of power that liberation theologians first reflected upon. It is also, in truth, a concept that feminist theologians have not entirely come to terms with. There is talk of mutuality and empowerment as though this would make power simply disappear or be miraculously transformed through erotic engagement with others. We know, through years of trying, that this is not the case. We are also left wondering whether women should be taking power in, and for, themselves. Of course, this would not be as an end in itself but it may be a necessary step along the way. This is a dangerous move if we believe that power corrupts.

The power of the enfleshed, narrative Christ lies in intimate connection and in the power that Heyward and others have called erotic. This raw, dynamic energy that exists within and between us is the power of Christ, the power that can burst out and transform. Of course, we have to understand ourselves as fully enfleshed if this power is to find its full expression since the impotency of metaphysics is always a danger in Christian theology. It seems entirely possible that what the early Christian writers were conveying about incarnation was not a once and for all event but the knowledge that unless we are fully in our bodies we will never be able to fully explore our divinity. Even the early fathers, influenced as they were by Greek dualism, understood that Jesus was most fully divine when he was most fully human, that Christ became man in order that all may become divine. I would like to change their emphasis but accept their vision. It was not the incarnation of the only son of God that allowed believers to achieve union with the divine, usually after death, but the bursting forth of the divine that makes it possible for all to grasp the same power 'anyone who makes an opening as he did wants others to enlarge it'.[6] The task for us all, then, is to bring the power of Christ to the forefront, to make empowered living the reality for all.

Perhaps when we grasp the power of erotic connection between us we will have collapsed the final barrier to empowerment that dualism sets in place, this barrier being our belief in the uniqueness of Christ. Viewing him as unique renders us powerless and is, in truth, as oppressive as any other patriarchal hierarchy.

For many Christians the power of Christ is seen to lie in the resurrection without which they would argue there is no Christianity. Once again there is a danger in announcing the resurrection as an event solely connected with the man Jesus. I understand the resurrection to be an important symbol, but I do not wish to imply that the raising of a particular body is what Christianity is about. Those who 'witnessed the resurrection' experienced the memory of the man and the power of the Christ of history, that is, the power to resist embedded in passionate and intimate connection. These accounts are later additions to the Gospels and can be seen in two ways, either as last-minute attempts to add weight to the argument or as reflections upon the power of Christ (as I am now defining it). If we take the latter view we see that groups of crushed and frightened individuals found, through shared memory and the weight of their circumstances, that the Christ is available in all times and places. This power is not lost with the person. Is it too outrageous to suggest that the story of transfiguration signalled the acceptance of the departure of the man Jesus but a personal embrace of the power of Christ that remains constant? Is that what the tongues of fire at Pentecost really symbolized, the passion and empowerment of accepting one's incarnation? Do we too need to experience a transfiguration, a letting go of the man, just as we are told Mary Magdalene was commanded to do, and a full embrace of the power that lies in the fibre of our beings?

This is no easy matter since we have been told religious tales that make us afraid of power, particularly embodied power. Eve is set before us as an example of how afraid we should really be since she interacted with the world in a truly sensual and embodied way taking joy as she did in the beauty of creation. The result was expulsion from paradise. Christian theology has viewed this as the tragedy that required the death of the son of God to atone for it, while Jewish theology views it as one step towards the fulfilment of creation. I wish to side with the Jewish interpretation in order to make the

---

6. Joan Casanas quoted in Pablo Richard, *The Idols of Death and the God of Life* (Maryknoll, NY: Orbis Books, 1982), p. 122.

point that paradise is not an ideal state to be in, it is unreal. As Mary Daly has pointed out, it is a walled-in confined space where freedom is limited. This is not an attractive prospect and is certainly not the sort of fulfilment of the power of God/Christ that I would hope for. Can we instead see Eve as the foremother of another tradition that encouraged engagement with the real stuff of life in order to enjoy its beauty, experience its power and risk its dangers? As Elisabeth Schüssler-Fiorenza has shown us, another tradition does exist in the Hebrew canon and that is the Sophia tradition in which she places Jesus, a tradition in which power is shared and in this way increased. How ironic that Jesus who shared the power of embodied wisdom with those around him has since been imaged as the sole power holder, the one who alone has saved the whole world.

Such an approach, through placing power amongst and within people, is accused of making redundant any notion of the transcendence of God/Christ. However, this is not entirely true, if we are able to think in terms of radical immanence rather than transcendence, which gives the impression of moving away. The radically immanent Christ is the one who increases in the sharing and therefore to some degree does transcend individual parts of the praxis. Through the power of intimate connection individuals are carried beyond their own limitations into a greater whole, yet they remain embodied and connected with themselves and with each other. Indeed, it is the connection that makes the expansion real and possible. I do not wish to limit this to humans, since connection with the earth is equally powerful because it too carries the dynamic power of creativity. It seems that Christianity as an incarnational religion has placed the emphasis on transcendence too strongly, which has resulted in a rather half-hearted engagement with the world by many Christians. Of course, it has also meant that promises of salvation have been viewed as absolute. Where would we find ourselves if we understood the crucifixion as a statement about the death of transcendence? After all, a truly transcendent God could avoid such a fate and the placing of the kingdom in the hands of humanity, a humanity that understands itself as divine by birth.

Forever and Ever?

I have outlined some problems with Christology and given some suggestions as to how we may continue to engage with it. But still the question remains, Will there be a feminist Christology in the future? However, looking at the question another way, can we afford to be without one? Carter Heyward has reminded us that, if we leave the discourse it does not mean that it crumbles but rather it remains in the hands of those who are perhaps most likely to misuse it. The symbols connected with Christology are powerful indeed, and so she, and Elisabeth Schüssler-Fiorenza, urge us not to give up. They claim that we have to keep contributing to the discourse or the Christo-fascist agenda will prevail. The result will be a world that thrives on dualism and the resultant exclusions that spring from such a way of thinking. We can, I think, understand their concerns a great deal more if we place them in the American context from which they spring. In Britain very few people attend church and fewer still would identify with a right-wing religious agenda. However, in America the Moral Majority makes up a vast number of voters who have a great deal of political clout and very rigid agendas. This is something that should concern us all given America's place in the world.[7] In addition Schüssler-Fiorenza does not want us to forfeit a heritage that is ours as much as anyone's. The winners write history, and if we leave the field of battle, we have conceded a victory to those who would write an exclusive history and create an even more divided world.

While Heyward and Schüssler-Fiorenza urge us to stay in the discourse, Daly, Christ and Hampson urge us to leave. Christ does point out that we have to make other symbols as powerful as those of the Christ, if we are to stop a decline into the old ways of thinking. While this is sound advice, it is also very hard to do, and it takes time for new ways of thinking to become commonplace, especially if they do not have cultural pegs on which to hang. They all argue that Christianity is too patriarchal and outmoded to make a difference in the world or to act as a positive environment for women. Christ argues that the Christ has not enhanced women's self-esteem or sense of worth, while Daly and Hampson highlight the ways in which the Christ figure has been used to torture, kill and otherwise suppress women.

So can women continue to interact with a figure that has historically been used against them? What place is there among the empowered daughters of Sophia for reflection on a once and for all son of God? Clearly there is no place, and certainly the feminist debate has moved us far beyond that point. Are we left looking for inspiration from a figure from long ago until such time as we can embrace the narrative and enflesh it in our own passionate living. When we become the Christ we profess to believe in, is there any place left for belief?

Christianity has at its heart the incarnation, a reality that has not really been dared by those who profess it. It also has as its working model the 'cataract

7. We should be all the more concerned since the events of 11th September 2001 and the moral rhetoric dividing the world between good and evil that has spewed out of the White House.

Christ' referred to earlier, that is, the Christ who is layered with class, gender, power, race and so much more. Feminist theology is scraping back the layers and with each layer finding more to challenge us. What does this say? I suspect that it means we will have to continue to make the Christ narrative supersede the reality of our lives for quite some time to come or we may lose the utopian vision that is so important to Christians and so necessary in the world of capitalist myopia in which we live. We are then, to use the jargon, in a place of realized eschatological tension, all that is, is here for the taking, but still remains to come. There are many more layers and many more fears to conquer before the awesome power of incarnation is grasped as lived experience by those who profess it. Indeed, at best how understanding appears to be partial, and so the spiralling nature of the Christ will remain alluring and demanding and we will remain passionately engaged in the revolution that is our Christic heritage.

BIBLIOGRAPHY

Althaus-Reid, Marcella, 'On wearing Skirts without Underwear: Indecent Theology Challenging the Liberation Theology of the Pueblo. Poor Women Contesting Christ', *Feminist Theology* 20 (1999), pp. 39-51.

Althaus-Reid, Marcella, 'The Indecency of Her Teaching: Notes for a Cureb Teaching of Feminist Theology in Europe', in Fiorenza and Copeland (eds.), *Feminist Theology*, pp. 133-40.

Aquino, Maria Pilar, 'Directions and Foundations of Hispanic/Latino Theology: Toward a Mestiza Theology of Liberation', in Arturo J. Banuelas (ed.), *Mestizo Christianity. Theology From a Latino Perspective:* (Maryknoll, NY: Orbis Books 1995), pp. 192-208.

Armstrong, Karen, *The Gospel According to Woman* (London: Pan, 1986).

Bingemar, Maria Clara, 'Women in the Future of the Theology of Liberation', in Ursula King, *Feminist Theology from the Third World* (London: SPCK, 1994), pp. 308-18.

Brock, Rita, *Journeys by Heart: A Christology of Erotic Power*, (New York: Crossroad, 1988).

Casanas, Joan, 'The Task of Making God Exist', in Pablo Richard (ed.), *The Idols of Death and the God of Life: A Theology.* (Maryknoll, NY: Orbis Books, 1983), pp. 130-41.

Christ, Carol, 'Why Women Need the Goddess: Phenomenological, Psychological and Political Reflections', in Christ, Carol and Judith Plaskow (eds.), *Womanspirit Rising* (San Francisco: Harper & Row, 1979), pp. 273-87.

Chung, Hyun Kyung, 'Han-pu-ri: Doing Theology from a Korean Woman's Perspective', in Virginia Fabella and Sun Ai Lee Park (eds.), *We Dare to Dream* (Hong Kong: AWCCT, 1989), pp. 60-72.

—*Struggle to Be the Sun Again* (London: SCM Press, 1990).

Crossan, John Dominic, *The Historical Jesus: The Life of a Mediterranean Peasant,* (San Francisco: HarperSanFrancisco, 1992).

Daly, Mary, *Beyond God the Father: Towards a Philosophy of Women's Liberation* (London: Women's Press, 1986).

—*Gyn/Ecology* (Boston: Beacon Press, 1978).

Deane-Drummond, Celia, 'Sophia: The Feminine Face of God as a Metaphor for an Ecotheology', *Feminist Theology* 16 (September 1997), pp. 11-31.

Douglas, Kelly Brown, *The Black Christ* (Maryknoll, NY: Orbis Books), 1994.

Eiesland, Nancy. *The Disabled God: Toward a Liberatory Theology of Disability* (Nashville: Abingdon Press, 1994).

Fabella, Virginia, 'Christology from an Asian woman's Perspective', in Fabella and Park, *We Dare To Dream*, pp. 109-113.

Fabella, Virginia, and Sun Ai Lee Park, *We Dare to Dream: Doing Theology as Asian Women* (Hong Kong: AWCCT, 1989).

Fiorenza, Elisabeth Schüssler, and Shawn Copeland (eds.), *Feminist Theology in Different Contexts* (London: SCM Press, 1996).

—*Violence against Women* (London: Concilium, 1994).

Gebara, Ivone 'A Cry for Life from Latin America', in K.C. Abraham and Bernadette Mbuy-Beya (eds.), *Spirituality of the Third World: A Cry for Life*, (Maryknoll, NY: Orbis Books, 1994), pp. 109-18.

—*Longing for Running Water:. Ecofeminism and Liberation* (Philadelphia: Fortress Press, 1999).

Gilligan, Carol, *In a Different Voice: Psychological Theory and Women's Development* (Cambridge, MA: Harvard University Press, 1982).

Gnanadason, Aruna, 'Women and Spirituality in Asia', in King, *Feminist Theology from the Third World*, pp. 351-60.

Green, Elisabeth, 'The Travail of Creation and the Daughters of God: Ecofeminism and Eschatology,' in *Feminist Theology* 14 (Sheffield: Sheffield Academic Press, 1994), pp. 44-56.

Grey, Mary, *Redeeming The Dream: Feminism, Redemption and Christian Tradition* (London: SPCK,1989).

—*The Wisdom of Fools? Seeking Revelation for Today* (London: SPCK, 1993).

Halkes, Catharina, *New Creation: Christian Feminism and the Renewal of the Earth* (London: SCM Press, 1991).

Hallman, David, *Ecotheology: Voices from South and North* (Maryknoll, NY: Orbis Books 1994).

Hampson, Daphne, *Swallowing a Fishbone? Feminist Theologians Debate Christianity* (London: SPCK, 1996).

Heyward, Carter, *Our Passion for Justice* (Cleveland, OH: Pilgrim Press, 1984).

—Saving Jesus from Those Who Are Right (Philadelphia: Fortress Press, 1999).

—The Redemption of God: A Theology of Mutual Relation, (Lanham, MD: University Press of America, 1982).

—'Touching our Strength. The Erotic as Power and the Love of God', (New York: HarperCollins, 1989).

Hinga, Teresa, 'Jesus Christ and the Liberation of Women in Africa', in King, *Feminist Theology from the Third World*, pp. 261-270.

Irigaray, Luce, This Sex which Is Not One (Ithaca, NY: Cornell University Press, 1985).

Isherwood, Lisa, *Liberating Christ* (Cleveland, OH: Pilgrim Press, 1999).

—'Marriage Haven or Hell: Twin Souls and Broken Bones', in Adrian Thatcher, *Celebrating Christian Marriage* (Edinburgh: T. & T. Clark, 2001).

Isherwood, Lisa and E. Stuart, *Introducing Body Theology*, (Sheffield: Sheffield Academic Press, 1998).

Johnson, Elisabeth, 'Redeeming the Name of Christ', in Catherine Mowry LaCugna (ed.), *Freeing Theology: The Essentials of Theology in Feminist Perspective.* (New York: Harper & Row, 1993), pp. 120-34.

—*She Who Is. The Mystery of God in Feminist Theological Discourse* (New York: Crossroad, 1994).

King, Ursula (ed.), *Feminist Theology from the Third World* (London, SPCK, 1994).

Kwok, Pui-Lan, 'Ecology and Christology', in *Feminist Theology* 15 (Sheffield: Sheffield Academic Press, 1997).

—'Jesus the Native', in Fernando F. Segovia and Mary Ann Tolbert (eds.), *Teaching the Bible: The Discourse and Politics of Biblical Pedagogy* (Maryknoll, NY: Orbis Books, 1998), pp. 69-85.

Lacan, Jacques, 'Jacques Lacan and the Ecole Freudienne', in Juliet Mitchell and Jacqueline Rose (eds./trans.), *Feminine Sexuality* (London: Macmillan Press, 1982).

Long, Asphodel, *In a Chariot Drawn by Lions* (London: Women's Press, 1991).

McFague, Sally, *Super Natural Christians: How We Should Love Nature* (London: SCM Press, 1997).

—*The Body of God: An Ecological Theology* (London, SCM Press, 1993).

Melancton, Monica, 'Christology and Women', in Fabella and Park, *We Dare to Dream*, pp. 14-22.

Moltmann-Wendel, Elisabeth, *A Land Flowing With Milk and Honey* (London: SCM Press, 1986).

Nasimuyu-Wasike, Anne, in Curt Codorette *et al.* (eds.), *An African Woman's Experience in Liberation Theology: An Introductory Reader* (Maryknoll, NY: Orbis Books, 1992).

Nim, Ahn Sang, 'Feminist Theology in the Korean Church', in Fabella and Park, *We Dare to Dream*, pp. 30-38.

Oduyoye, Mercy Amba, *Introducing African Women's Theology* (Sheffield: Sheffield Academic Press, 2001).

Ortner, Sherry, 'Is Female to Male as Nature Is to Culture?', in Michelle Zimbalist Rosaldo and Louise Lamphere (eds.), in *Women Culture and Society* (Stanford, Stanford University Press, 1974), pp. 67-87.

Patai, Raphael, *The Hebrew Goddess*, New York, Avon Books, 1978.

Pirani, Alix, *The Absent Mother Restoring the Goddess to Judaism and Christianity* (London: Mandala, 1991).

Primavesi, Anne, *From Apocalypse to Genesis: Ecology, Feminism and Christianity* (Tunbridge Wells: Burns & Oates, 1991).

Richard, Pablo, *The Idols of Death and the God of Life* (Maryknoll, NY: Orbis Books, 1982).

Ritchie, Nelly, 'Women and Christology', in Elsa Tamaz (ed.) *Through Her Eyes: Women's Theology from Latin America* (Maryknoll, NY: Orbis Books, 1989), pp. 79-91.

Ruether, Rosemary, *Gaia and God: An Ecofeminist Theology of Earth Healing* (San Francisco: Harper & Row, 1992).

—*Introducing Redemption in Christian Feminism* (Sheffield: Sheffield Academic Press, 1998).

—'Motherearth and The Megamachine: A Theology of Liberation in a Feminine, Somatic and Ecological Perspective', in Carol Christ (ed.), *Womanspirit Rising* (San Francisco: Harper & Row, 1979), pp. 43-53.

—*Sexism And God-Talk* (London: SCM Press, 1983).

—*To Change the World: Christology and Cultural Criticism* (New York: Crossroad, 1988).

—*Women Healing Earth* (London: SCM Press, 1996).

Russell, Letty, *Human Liberation from a Feminist Perspective: A Theology* (Philadelphia: Westminster Press, 1974).

Schüssler-Fiorenza, Elisabeth, *In Memory of Her* (London: SCM Press, 1983).

—*Jesus: Miriam's Son, Sophia's Prophet*, (New York: Continuum, 1994).

Schweitzer, Albert, *The Quest of the Historical Jesus: A Critical Study of its Progress From Reimarus to Wrede* (London: A. & C. Black, 1922).

Soelle, D., *Theology for Sceptics: Reflections on God* (Philadelphia: Fortress Press, 1995).

Souga, Therese, 'The Christ Event from the Viewpoint of African Women', in Fabella and Mercy Amba Oduyoye, *With Passion and Compassion* (Maryknoll, NY: Orbis Books, 1994), pp. 22-29.

Southard, Naomi F., 'Recovery and Rediscovered Images: Spiritual Resources for Asian American Women', in King, *Feminist Theology from the Third World*, pp. 378-91.

Stone, Merlin, 'The Three Faces of Goddess Spirituality', in C. Spretnak (ed.), *The Politics of Women's Spirituality* (New York: Doubleday, 1982), pp. 118-28.

—*When God Was a Woman* (New York: Harvester; HBJ Books, 1976).

Stuart, Elisabeth, 'Disruptive Bodies. Disability, Embodiment and Sexuality', in Lisa Isherwood, *The Good News of the Body: Sexual Theology and Feminism*, (Sheffield: Sheffield Academic Press, 2000), pp. 166-184.

Tamez, Elsa, 'Quetzalcoatl y El Dios Cristiano' *Cuadernos de Teologia y Cultura* 6 (1992), pp. 5-13.

Thistlewaite, Susan Brocks', Every Two Minutes', in Judith Plaskow and Carol Christ, *Weaving the Visions: New Patterns in Feminist Spirituality* (New York: HarperCollins, 1989).

Tinker, George, 'Jesus, Corn Mother and Conquest', in Jace Weaver (ed.), *Native American Religious Identity* (Maryknoll, NY: Orbis Books, 1998), pp. 134-54.

Von Kellenbach, Katharina, 'Overcoming the Teaching of Contempt', in Athalya Brenner and Carole Fontain (eds.), *A Feminist Companion to Reading the Bible: Approaches, Methods and Strategies* (Sheffield: Sheffield Academic Press, 1997), pp. 41-53.

Walker, Alice, *Possessing the Secret of Joy* (New York: Harcourt Brace Jovanovich, 1993).

Westermann, C., *Creation* (London: SPCK, 1974).

Williams, Delores, 'Black Women's Surrogate Experience and the Christian Notion of Redemption', in William Eakin, Jay B. McDaniel and Paula Cooey (eds.), *After Patriarchy: Feminist Transformations of the World Religions* (Maryknoll, NY: Orbis Books, 1991), pp. 10-22.

—*Sisters in the Wilderness: The Challenge of Womanist God-Talk* (Maryknoll, NY: Orbis Books, 1993).

INDEX

INDEX OF REFERENCES

Index of Authors

FEMINIST THEOLOGY TITLES

Individual Titles in Feminist Theology
Linda Hogan, *From Women's Experience to Feminist Theology*
Lisa Isherwood and Dorothea McEwan (eds.), *An A–Z of Feminist Theology*
Lisa Isherwood and Dorothea McEwan, *Introducing Feminist Theology*
Kathleen O'Grady, Ann L. Gilroy and Janette Patricia Gray (eds.), *Bodies, Lives, Voices: Gender in Theology*
Melissa Raphael, *Thealogy and Embodiment: The Post-Patriarchal Reconstruction of Female Sacrality*
Deborah Sawyer and Diane Collier (eds.), *Is There a Future for Feminist Theology?*
Lisa Isherwood (ed.), *The Good News of the Body: Sexual Theology and Feminism*
Alf Hiltebeitel and Kathleen M. Erndl, *Is the Goddess a Feminist? The Politics of South Asian Goddesses*

Introductions in Feminist Theology
Rosemary Ruether, *Introducing Redemption in Christian Feminism*
Lisa Isherwood and Elizabeth Stuart, *Introducing Body Theology*
Melissa Raphael, *Introducing Thealogy: Discourse on the Goddess*
Pui-lan Kwok, *Introducing Asian Feminist Theology*
Janet H. Wootton, *Introducing a Practical Feminist Theology of Worship*
Mary Grey, *Introducing Feminist Images of God*
Mercy Amba Oduyoye, *Introducing African Women's Theology*
Lisa Isherwood, *Introducing Feminist Christologies*

Feminist Companion to the Bible (1st Series)
Athalya Brenner (ed.), *A Feminist Companion to the Song of Songs*
Athalya Brenner (ed.), *A Feminist Companion to Genesis*
Athalya Brenner (ed.), *A Feminist Companion to Ruth*
Athalya Brenner (ed.), *A Feminist Companion to Judges*
Athalya Brenner (ed.), *A Feminist Companion to Samuel–Kings*
Athalya Brenner (ed.), *A Feminist Companion to Exodus–Deuteronomy*
Athalya Brenner (ed.), *A Feminist Companion to Esther, Judith and Susanna*
Athalya Brenner (ed.), *A Feminist Companion to the Latter Prophets*
Athalya Brenner (ed.), *A Feminist Companion to the Wisdom Literature*
Athalya Brenner (ed.), *A Feminist Companion to the Hebrew Bible in the New Testament*
Athalya Brenner and Carole Fontaine (eds.), *A Feminist Companion to Reading the Bible: Approaches, Methods and Strategies*

Feminist Companion to the Bible (2nd Series)
Athalya Brenner and Carole Fontaine (eds.), *Wisdom and Psalms*
Athalya Brenner (ed.), *Genesis*
Athalya Brenner (ed.), *Judges*
Athalya Brenner (ed.), *Ruth and Esther*
Athalya Brenner (ed.), *Samuel and Kings*
Athalya Brenner (ed.), *Exodus–Deuteronomy*
Athalya Brenner (ed.), *Prophets and Daniel*